"If you've ever struggled to maintain daily Bible reading, questioned the importance of regular prayer, or faltered in your efforts to commit to the local church, this book is for you. In other words, this book is for all of us—for who doesn't sometimes need a good friend to remind us of the value of healthy spiritual habits and point us to the everlasting treasure that awaits? In the pages of *Everyday Faithfulness*, Glenna Marshall is that friend. She comes alongside readers with personal testimony, biblical truth, warm encouragement, and an occasional, well-placed elbow when we need it most. Whether you've been a Christian for days or decades, this book will equip you to persevere and, in the process, find joy."

Megan Hill, author, *Praying Together* and *A Place to Belong*; Editor, The Gospel Coalition

"*Everyday Faithfulness* is a wonderful gift for Christian women who long for encouragement to walk closely with their Lord throughout life's challenges and joys. Glenna Marshall approaches our need for ordinary perseverance with conviction, grace, and great hope in our faithful Savior. She offers us a fresh look at the many opportunities we're given to live like we belong to Christ, today and every day. *Everyday Faithfulness* is what we all need, and these words will spur you on through every season in your own walk with Jesus."

Bethany Barendregt, Content Director and Podcast Host, *Women Encouraged*

"Every Christian wants to be faithful. Unfortunately, many of us are really more concerned with the results of faithfulness than with the ordinary plodding and perseverance of daily faithfulness itself. Glenna Marshall writes to encourage us in the midst of this everyday perseverance. Her writing is a blend of humble transparency and biblical insight, all written in the voice of a trusted friend. I'm so thankful for her and for *Everyday Faithfulness*. What a gift to the church!"

Jaquelle Crowe Ferris, author, *This Changes Everything: How the Gospel Transforms the Teen Years*

"When it comes to spiritual growth, we're often hoping for big changes to happen overnight. While we may long for a fast sprint toward holiness, Glenna Marshall reminds us that spiritual growth usually consists of ordinary moments of everyday faithfulness. *Everyday Faithfulness* is a needed and encouraging book that points us to the joy of walking with God one day at a time, one step at a time."

Melissa B. Kruger, Director of Women's Initiatives, The Gospel Coalition; author, *Growing Together*

Everyday Faithfulness

Gospel Coalition Books from Crossway

Everyday Faithfulness

The Beauty of Ordinary Perseverance
in a Demanding World

Glenna Marshall

:: CROSSWAY®

WHEATON, ILLINOIS

Published in association with the literary agency of Wolgemuth & Associates, Inc.

Cover image and design: Crystal Courtney

First printing 2020

Printed in the United States of America

Scripture quotations are from the ESV® Bible (The Holy Bible, English Standard Version®), copyright © 2001 by Crossway, a publishing ministry of Good News Publishers. Used by permission. All rights reserved.

All emphases in Scripture quotations have been added by the author.

Trade paperback ISBN: 978-1-4335-6729-2
ePub ISBN: 978-1-4335-6732-2
PDF ISBN: 978-1-4335-6730-8
Mobipocket ISBN: 978-1-4335-6731-5

Library of Congress Cataloging-in-Publication Data

Names: Marshall, Glenna, author.
Title: Everyday faithfulness : the beauty of ordinary perseverance in a demanding world / Glenna Marshall.
Description: Wheaton, Illinois : Crossway, [2020] | Series: Gospel coalition | Includes bibliographical references and index. | Summary: "Examines various seasons of life when faithfulness to Christ is hard, and shows what daily perseverance looks like"— Provided by publisher.
Identifiers: LCCN 2019038698 (print) | LCCN 2019038699 (ebook) | ISBN 9781433567292 (trade paperback) | ISBN 9781433567308 (pdf) | ISBN 9781433567315 (mobi) | ISBN 9781433567322 (epub)
Subjects: LCSH: Faith. | Christian life. | Perseverance (Ethics) | Persistence—Religious aspects—Christianity.
Classification: LCC BV4637 .M3185 2020 (print) | LCC BV4637 (ebook) | DDC 248.4—dc23
LC record available at https://lccn.loc.gov/2019038698
LC ebook record available at https://lccn.loc.gov/2019038699

Crossway is a publishing ministry of Good News Publishers.

VP		31	30	29	28	27	26	25	24	23	22	21
14	13	12	11	10	9	8	7	6	5	4	3	2

For Leota, whose everyday faithfulness
has encouraged me in mine.
I miss your quiet presence on the pew behind me at church.

Contents

Think Like a Farmer

In the humid, mosquito-thick summers of Southeast Missouri where I've lived for the past fifteen years, I've attempted to grow a vegetable garden exactly once. My next-door neighbor Bob, a retiree who used to run his own landscaping business, leaned over the adjoining fence one day and watched while I staked out the square allotted for my future cornucopia of summer produce. "I'll bring my tiller over and chew up that dirt for you, if you want," he offered.

Throughout the late spring and early summer, he volunteered bits of advice while I planted tomatoes, peppers, and squash—and pretended I knew what I was doing. He'd lean across the fence and make suggestions for keeping the squirrels out, for protecting against pop-up thunderstorms, for the best times to water when rain was scarce. I did everything Bob said, but I quickly discovered that I didn't have the patience for gardening. I hated the heat, the bugs, and the incessant need for weeding. I especially hated the weeks of waiting for plants to break through the earth, grow, blossom, and then turn out vegetables. I mean, I could just drive to the grocery store and *buy* some tomatoes, right?

Though I was thrilled by the first vegetables we picked and ate, I quickly lost interest in the work, and my garden grew wild. By that time, the tomatoes had failed anyway. At the end of the season, I uprooted everything and tossed the leavings in the brush pile. We intended to carry off the brush in the fall, but we didn't get around to it until the next summer. That's when I discovered two sturdy tomato plants growing in the wild stack of fallen tree branches and compost. I was a bit resentful. The tomatoes that wouldn't grow under my watering, weeding, and mulching were flourishing in a forgotten pile of garbage. Their green stems heavy with plump, red orbs mocked me.

I'm certain Bob laughed at me too each time he ducked back behind the fence to head indoors. My patience for the slow growth of summer vegetables was thin, and he knew it. I didn't want to do the work, and he knew it. What I did want was fruit without the investment, the life of a gardener without actually gardening, and Bob knew it all.

In his epistle, James encourages believers to be patient until the Lord returns. Since Christ's ascension, his people have believed he will return for his church, and that he will present her pure and spotless before the Father. Jesus's brother left us the encouragement to be steadfast while we wait for the day of Christ's appearing. Under the inspiration of the Holy Spirit, James turns our impatient hearts to the farmer and says, "Be patient, therefore, brothers until the coming of the Lord. See how the farmer waits for the precious fruit of the earth, being patient about it, until it receives the early and the late rains. You also, be patient. Establish your hearts, for the coming of the Lord is at hand" (James 5:7–8).

When my husband and I first moved to our Missouri farming community, I was surprised by how the fields of crops leaned into the city limits. A bank in the middle of town might be flanked by a cotton field one year and a cornfield the next. Crop rotation is something I've turned into a yearly guessing game, and seasonal field-burning always sends me to bed with raging allergies.

I'll never forget my first midweek prayer meeting at the church where my husband serves as pastor. One of the members stood to pray at the end of the service. I remember his prayer distinctly because I was struck with its simplicity and humility: he prayed for us to follow Christ faithfully, and he prayed for rain. At least two congregants at the time were full-time farmers, and their livelihoods depended on summer rains. Not too much and not too little. Every year, they waited patiently and trusted the Lord to provide for their fields of cotton, rice, corn, and soybeans. I always think of that prayer when I read James's encouragement to be faithful like farmers. Faithfulness by definition calls us to be loyal, steadfast, constant, and reliable. But outside the agrarian corners of the world, we struggle to model our spiritual faithfulness after farmers waiting for rain like their lives depend on it.

Life or death. That's what we're talking about here.

Like my experience with a small twenty-by-twenty-foot garden, following Christ with everyday faithfulness—doing the work of perseverance while also trusting God to work—can feel like an endless endeavor with slow-yielding results. The devices we chain ourselves to for knowledge, connection, and entertainment do not require that we wait or try very hard. We press buttons or give voice commands, and the world rushes to our fingertips. If the Wi-Fi is poor, we bristle with impatience. If the content on one site bores us, we click over to another. Our culture does not aid us in the discipline of perseverance, and yet God calls us to persevere in faithfulness to him. Jesus said, "The one who endures to the end will be saved" (Matt. 10:22). The farmer's perseverance keeps his fields irrigated and free from pests so the crops are pleased to grow. The Christian's perseverance keeps her life rooted in the habits and practices that keep her near the Father's side so that her spiritual maturity is pleased to grow.

Perseverance reveals the fruit of true, saving faith. It is both an exercise of genuine faith and evidence of it. Perseverance doesn't save us, but it reveals that we have been saved. Paul charged young pastor Timothy to persist in sharing the message of the gospel whether or not it was convenient (2 Tim. 4:2). This is the underpinning of true faithfulness: persistence whether or not it is convenient. Faithfulness in following Christ isn't optional for true believers. Whatever seasons we find ourselves in this side of heaven, God still calls us to faithfulness. Perseverance in Christ is our daily work. A steadfast grip on the gospel is still God's charge to us even when our schedules are full, our trials are many, or our days are mundane.

Faithfulness is an everyday calling. It's regular, it's ordinary, it's taking a really long view of the Christian life. It's reshaping our desires for immediate fruit and committing to following Jesus for the long haul. It's getting up every single day and believing that God is your treasure, that the gospel of Jesus is worth your every breath, and that he is enough. Faithfulness is doing this again tomorrow and the next day and ten years from now. Faithfulness is ordinary. It's unremarkable. It plods. It is also precious in the sight of the God who works out lifelong sanctifying perseverance in your life for your good and his glory.

Everyday faithfulness requires patience and fortitude that's desperately dependent upon God's own faithfulness to us. Yet the fruit, the harvest, the return for our everyday plodding is worth more than all the days, months, and years of our long-haul perseverance. When Christ is our daily treasure during the seasons that challenge our steadfastness, we'll reap the benefits of being safely fastened to his side during every shifting shadow and change in life. We'll know him more through his word. Our love for him will increase as our love for sin decreases. We'll look to him more and more, and our regular beholding of his glorious nature will in turn cause others to look to him more. We'll be well-suited for a lifetime of living and longing for Jesus to be our greatest treasure and our deepest joy.

The plodding may last for a lifetime, but the glory will last forever.

Faithful Like . . .

At the end of each chapter, I'll share about the faithfulness of a woman who has encouraged me with her perseverance in regard to the subject matter of the particular chapter. These are real people who have lived the very definition of everyday faithfulness with no accolades, applause, or notoriety. They are not famous, nor do they seek to be. They are everyday, regular people like you and me. Some are still living, and some are now with Christ. May their everyday faithfulness encourage you in yours.

1

What Is Everyday Faithfulness?

"I don't know what's wrong with me," I confessed to my friend. She raised her eyebrows, took a sip of coffee, and silently beckoned me to continue. I'd just shared that I hadn't touched my Bible in weeks, maybe longer. It was something I'd confessed to her many times in the past. "I know I have no excuse. I know that Christians are supposed to read the Bible regularly. I just can't seem to get into a good routine. I do pray sometimes, but you know—sporadically." My friend nodded but didn't reply.

"Maybe I'm just too busy," I said with a sigh. My words fell flat between us; we both saw it for the excuse that it was. I knew my friend had a regular habit of waking at six o'clock in the morning to read the Bible before her kids got up. I felt guilty just sitting in the same room with her. Her discipline seemed to cast a spotlight on my lack of it. "I want to be *eager* to read Scripture. Maybe then I wouldn't feel so disconnected from the Lord all the time," I told my friend.

My friend wisely responded the way she always did—with a gentle encouragement to start fresh tomorrow. I knew starts and stops were better than nothing, but I didn't want to be sitting in her living room ten years later having the same conversation. Still, I held on to a thin strand of hope that someday I'd drift toward maturity in Christ. Someday.

Later, during a prolonged season of difficult trials, I found myself unprepared for suffering. In desperation I began to seek the Lord in Scripture, and, slowly, the habit of reaching for my Bible every morning began to change my life. I often thank the Lord for the trials that sent me to his word because I know now that I would never have run toward Christ otherwise.

We've All Been Her

As a pastor's wife, I've heard many similar confessions from women who, like me, have tried desperately to get their spiritual acts together apart from regular Bible reading, prayer, and corporate worship. I've witnessed one friend live in continual defeat and regret over long lapses of any kind of spiritual discipline. I've watched another friend spend many years hoping that when life settles down, she'll finally find a routine of daily faithfulness to Christ—only to discover yet another sharp bend in the road to keep her from it. I know now that unless we all commit to regular, daily faithfulness to Christ, we'll be confessing our prayerlessness and dusty Bible covers for years to come to another believer who's heard it many, many times before.

I see her all the time—the Christian woman who wants to follow Jesus but can't seem to get past life's hurdles to know him in his word. She's everywhere. She's the accountability partners, the Bible study members, the church visitors who never make it past the first meeting. She's the woman who has gradually tapered down church attendance in favor of weekends at the lake, ball tournaments, or leisurely Sunday mornings spent prioritizing biological familial ties over spiritual ones. She's the person who thinks one day she'll wake up holier without having fed the faithfulness that holiness requires. She's me, and, likely, she's been you.

Many of us long to follow Jesus more closely, but we are more focused on our present circumstances than on a long view of faithfulness. We want visible change after a week of Bible reading or a month of church attendance. We desire instant returns for our minimal efforts, but a lifetime marked by steadfast faith doesn't happen overnight. It's built upon years and months of many ordinary days of ordinary perseverance. Though beautiful when traced in decades of retrospect, faithfulness is unremarkable in real-time practice. Daily and weekly spiritual disciplines require common exercises like frequent alarm-setting for Bible reading and getting to church on time for corporate worship. Diligent, unremarkable practices make way for lifelong spiritual growth. We practice perseverance today—every single today—so that we can practice perseverance ten, twenty, and thirty years from now.

We've all had seasons of life when investing in our relationship with Christ has taken a back seat to work, parenting, health, and relationships. We might justify it—*as long as I still believe the gospel now, I can get to growth later*. I used to live with this kind of mature future faithfulness in mind. I thought I'd become more disciplined when I was older, when the kids were older, when I had more life experience, when life wasn't so busy. It was like expecting my garden to be free of weeds and full of vegetables without ever stepping outdoors to tend it.

God expects spiritual growth in every believer—it's proof we've tasted that the Lord is good (1 Pet. 2:3). But there's no switch that flips when we suddenly reach maturity. Expecting to wake up holy some morning in the future is folly if we aren't vigilant in following Christ *this* morning. Faithfulness

to Christ, the kind that perseveres to the end, comes in persevering to the end of *today*.

God has given us the means we need to persevere today,
twenty years from now, and all the days in between. Through
his word, prayer, and the church, we are equipped to draw near
to God, hold fast to our confession of faith, and remain rooted
in truth through the people of God. We'll talk about the importance of these regular expressions of faith in the next chapter,
but it's these gifts from God that ready us for lifelong faithfulness no matter what seasons we encounter.

The most faithful saints I have known and loved all have
had the same trait: a determination to follow Jesus more today
than yesterday. These people don't have advanced degrees or
illustrious careers. You won't read about them in magazines
or spot them on the red carpet. They're regular folks: car sales-
men, bank tellers, stay-at-home moms, insurance agents,
teachers, nurses, retirees. But they are people who studied
their Bibles daily, prayed without ceasing, and showed up at
church every Sunday. Their professions of faith were publicly
proclaimed through baptism and inwardly examined at the
Lord's Table. They grew in maturity as they fed their faithfulness regularly. They are proof that our daily decisions to follow
Christ closely are incredibly important for our perseverance in
the faith. Perhaps more than we realize.

Swerving from the Truth

A few names in the New Testament make me nervous, like
Alexander, Hymenaeus, and Philetus. Don't get me wrong,
they're nice names (well, the first one is). But the stories behind
these men are sobering when we consider what they teach us
about following Christ. We don't know a lot about them, but
what we do know is alarming. Paul mentioned Hymenaeus

and Philetus by name when he warned Timothy that mishandling God's word leads to false teaching. The gangrenous effect of heresy had upset the faith of others when, Paul explained, these men "swerved from the truth" (2 Tim. 2:18). Paul also mentioned that Alexander with Hymenaeus had rejected the faith. As a result of their apostasy, Paul "handed [them] over to Satan that they may learn not to blaspheme" (1 Tim. 1:20). Tampering with the truth of the gospel has grave consequences. These men had rejected God's truth and the church's protection of it. If they had been faithful followers of Christ at one point, how did they slip downward into blasphemy?

Paul captured it in a phrase: they swerved from the truth. We put our souls in danger when we wander outside the safety of connectedness within the church and lose the truth of Scripture. The regular teaching and intake of Scripture in the community of faith protects us against falling away. The author of Hebrews tells us to "exhort one another every day, as long as it is called 'today,' that none of you may be hardened by the deceitfulness of sin. For we have come to share in Christ, if indeed we hold our original confidence firm to the end" (Heb. 3:13–14). The church is vital in offering protection for our souls and helping us hold on to the truth of the gospel. Paul told young pastor Timothy to devote himself to the public reading of Scripture, to immerse himself in it, and to persist in keeping a close watch on himself (1 Tim. 4:13–16). While this was pastoral advice, there is great wisdom here for us. Persistent, regular exposure to Scripture and consistent connection to the church anchor our faith. Vigilance matters because the enemy wants to devour what he can.

Perhaps the stories of Alexander, Hymenaeus, and Philetus seem like overstated warnings of something unlikely to happen to us, but the truth is that without regular Bible intake, communion with the Lord in prayer, and connection to the church, it's easier to swerve from the truth than you might think. It might not be as obvious in your life as it was in theirs. It might not take the form of embracing false teaching. It might look like nothing more than a reluctance to hold on to the things that keep us attached to Christ. But it is still the path that leads to death.

I've observed all kinds of people who either were never truly converted or whose profession of faith in Christ was smothered beneath the stress and strains of life. Countless predators and distractions are ready to gobble up our faithfulness after the gospel seed has been sown (Matt. 13:1–23). Some obstacles are so effective at scraping away anything appearing like perseverance that all that's left is a nominal faith at best, which really isn't faith at all.

Here's the thing about true saving faith: it will always be evidenced by continued faithfulness to Christ. And that's what we *don't* see in Alexander, Hymenaeus, or Philetus—continued faithfulness. The way we distinguish good soil from bad soil in Jesus's parable of the sower is by the evidence of fruit that grows in it. Faithfulness is proof of life. Jesus said it succinctly: "By your endurance you will gain your lives" (Luke 21:19). Jesus wasn't talking about gaining physical lives but rather eternal ones. Perseverance reveals that the profession of faith was real, and it will result in real life with him in heaven. Paul said it similarly: "If we endure, we will also reign with him" (2 Tim. 2:12).

Faithfulness to Christ isn't a one-time decision. It cannot be sequestered to a faded memory of standing next to a pastor in front of a church and signing your name to a membership card. Nor can it depend on mountaintop experiences like conferences or concerts for nourishment. It can't breathe between tiny spurts of Bible reading or emergency prayers. It can't grow disconnected from the truth of Scripture, and it is unlikely to flourish apart from the body of Christ.

Faithfulness to Christ is a daily, lifelong pursuit. A lifetime of daily faithfulness will be full of unremarkable single days of faithfulness. And what encourages us to be steadfast on a daily basis is keeping an eye on this lifelong perseverance Jesus spoke of in Matthew 24:13. Rather than fading from following him because our love has grown cold, "the one who endures to the end will be saved."

Like anything that blossoms and produces fruit, faithfulness requires daily sustenance to grow. If you want to ensure that you'll still be reading your Bible and carving out time to pray each day ten years from now, then you must begin making it a daily practice now. If you want to make certain that you don't drift from the church when you're older, then make sure you're invested in the body of Christ now. Today's efforts aren't just for today! They're for tomorrow and next week and next month and five years from now. If you want to guarantee that you don't swerve from the truth someday, build your life around practices that keep you connected to Christ, his gospel, and his church.

Faithfulness to Christ requires dying to your desires every single day and instead submitting them to what pleases God. Faithfulness requires us to release our clenched fists, letting the love of entertainment, comfort, and laziness fall through our fingers, and watching it shatter, confident that God can bring good from our efforts at killing sin. It means believing that when Jesus died on the cross, he really did break the power of sin over you, so you are free to fight sin instead of catering to it. Faithfulness requires that we construct our days around the disciplines of Bible reading, prayer, and investment in the body of Christ rather than fitting those things in when we can.

If we want our lives to be marked by steadfastness to Christ, then we can find comfort in knowing God has equipped us to that end. Beginning is as uncomplicated as getting up in the morning to read your Bible, and then doing the same thing the next day after that. And the day after that. Uncomplicated, but not always easy. Regular, everyday faithfulness to Christ doesn't usually bring about fame or praise. No one is clapping when you roll out of bed a half hour earlier to pray or when you spend your lunch break reading your Bible, but you will grow in wisdom and in nearness to Christ as you persevere. You won't get a raise when you leave work early to attend the midweek prayer service at church, but you will be knit tightly with other believers who are also walking a steadfast path with Christ. The accolades are few when you turn off the television to work on Scripture memory before bed, yet you'll find that God's word has the power to change the way you think. Everyday faithfulness feels ordinary because it should be ordinary for the believer. It's expected, but it must be fed every single day to thrive. Faithfulness to Christ recognizes that the miracle of salvation continues in the miracle of sanctification. We are dependent upon God's grace for both.

As faithfulness blooms and grows in your life, it will become a way of life, and it will bring about deep joy that cannot be eclipsed by the ordinariness of your days. The culmination of individual days of faithfulness results in a lifetime of following Jesus and becoming like him. Following Jesus will *be* your life!

The Intersection of God's Sovereignty and Our Perseverance

Thankfully, the maturity of a steadfast heart that reflects the image of your Savior and clings to the truth doesn't weigh on only your shoulders. You've likely heard theologians, pastors, or church members debate the tension between God's sovereignty and man's responsibility. Hopefully, you've heard it debated kindly and with proper use of Scripture. When it comes to perseverance and faithfulness in the life of the believer, the same question looms large before us. Do we persevere or does God persevere us?

Well, *yes*. The apostle Paul encouraged the first-century Christians in Philippi, and us by extension, to obey the Lord and to "work out your own salvation with fear and trembling, for it is God who works in you, both to will and to work for his good pleasure" (Phil. 2:12–13). I don't think Paul is speaking out of both sides of his mouth here. He's saying yes to both. We are commanded to work out our salvation, to persevere in the faith, to obey the commands of Christ *while recognizing* that it is God who works in us to do those things. Any desire to be holy, any inclination to obey, any hope anchored in him comes *from* him and is initiated *by* him. We obey God and credit him for our obedience.

When we repent and believe in order to be saved, we do so because God predestined us for salvation, called us, justified us, and will one day glorify us (see Rom. 8:30). When it comes to following Christ between justification and glorification (that long journey we call sanctification), we obey him *and* we acknowledge that he gives us the will and follow-through to obey. The Godhead is personally invested in your faithfulness! John Piper says:

> If you are persevering in faith today, you owe it to the blood of Jesus. The Holy Spirit, who is working in you to preserve your faith, is honoring the purchase of Jesus. God the Spirit works in us what God the Son obtained for us. The Father planned it. Jesus bought it. The Spirit applies it—all of them infallibly.[1]

---

1. John Piper. "Eternal Security Is a Community Project," Desiring God website, September 15, 2012, https://www.desiringgod.org/messages/eternal-security-is-a-community-project—2/.

Paul gives us the purpose of working out our salvation and recognizing God's work in it in Philippians 2:14–16: "Do all things without grumbling or disputing, *that* you may be blameless and innocent, children of God without blemish in the midst of a crooked and twisted generation, among whom you shine as lights in the world, holding fast to the word of life." Here is the purpose in our everyday faithfulness: *to know him and to make him known*. Perhaps it seems a daunting endeavor to shine perpetually bright in a world dark with hostility toward the gospel and the people of God. But faithfulness leans into the world while keeping us from becoming like it. Holding firmly to the message of life every day ensures that we do not deviate from it.

Everyday faithfulness is a protection from reverting back to the life you lived before Jesus saved you, from abandoning faith in him when life takes a hard turn, from accepting a false gospel in a world of tantalizing but twisted versions of it. Reorienting our hearts to the truths of Scripture each day keeps us aligned with that purpose of knowing and making him known. Meeting with the body of Christ on a regular basis holds us accountable and encourages our faith. Individual and corporate spiritual disciplines are tools for knowing Christ better on a daily and weekly basis. These tools equip us to point others to Christ as well. Speaking the gospel message to our unbelieving friends and family requires that we live in a manner that upholds our claim that Jesus is worth our very lives. Faithful evangelism assumes we know well the one we are sharing with our lost neighbors and family members.

Yes, it's weighty to know that so much of our spiritual trajectory hangs on our perseverance. But this is where Paul's follow-up statement to his exhortation to "work out" is so glorious. It's *God* who is working in your perseverance! Paul uses similar language in Colossians when he explains that presenting everyone mature in Christ is his goal. He says, "For this I toil, struggling with all his energy that he powerfully works within me" (Col. 1:29). Paul labored for the maturity of believers, but he did so with Christ's energy that worked powerfully in him. Paul's labor, Christ's energy and power.

And here's more good news to encourage you: God has promised to preserve those who are his, and he always keeps his promises. If you are working out your salvation with fear and trembling, then be comforted knowing you are not in any way doing it alone. He is working in you, enabling you to remain faithful. If you belong to him, no one can pluck you out of his hand (see John 10:27–29). You will persevere because he has purposed to finish the good work he began. "I am sure of this, that he who began a good work in you will bring it to completion at the day of Jesus Christ" (Phil. 1:6).

If all of this is true, how do we "work out" our faithfulness when so many predators and distractions are out to thwart our perseverance? The suffering, hostility, and apathy we face on this fallen planet will require us to be vigilant in every season. There will never be a season of our sanctification when we will casually arrive at holiness. Following isn't passive, and it isn't drifting. Following Christ assumes action.

Follow Means Follow

Following Christ means *following* him. It means emulating him, learning to be like him, responding like he would, taking up his message and sharing it, obeying him, and expecting the world to respond to you in the way it responded to him. If you've read the Gospels closely, you know that following Jesus leads to some hard places in life. The New Testament writers paradoxically called it *blessing* to share in the sufferings of Christ. They knew that intimacy with the Savior grows from clinging to him when life is unraveling at the seams. It thrives when we latch on to his promise to be faithful though our hearts ache with longing or our bodies pulse with pain. Nearness to Christ is joy when our days are bursting with busyness.

Suffering, waiting, fear, busyness, plodding in anonymity—these are not times to waste in apathy or wishful thinking about future sanctification. These are pressing opportunities to share in Christ's sufferings by clinging to him tightly. If we follow faithfully only when life is free of trouble, we will value only that trouble-free existence. But if we fasten ourselves to Christ when life is a sinking ship, then we learn to treasure him as our anchor. We discover that our faithfulness is tethered to his, especially during the troubling seasons of life.

When I look back at the last twenty years of my life, I see only a few stretches of what I'd call ease. If we spend only the tranquil days of our sanctification seeking Christ, then we will have long periods of life when we're not trusting him, knowing him, or making him known. And because this world is broken down with sin, your life might be marked by more long, hard winters than carefree springs.

We must be vigilant because our hearts will not casually become more holy while we sit around and do nothing to feed our faithfulness. My expectation to arrive at spiritual maturity someday was dangerous. D. A. Carson words it well:

> People do not drift toward holiness. Apart from grace-driven effort, people do not gravitate toward godliness, prayer, obedience to Scripture, faith, and delight in the Lord. We drift toward compromise and call it tolerance; we drift toward disobedience and call it freedom; we drift toward superstition and call it faith. We cherish the indiscipline of lost self-control and call it relaxation; we slouch

toward prayerlessness and delude ourselves into thinking we have escaped legalism; we slide toward godlessness and convince ourselves we have been liberated.[2]

This side of heaven, we always struggle to grow in godliness and to feed our faithfulness. On the easiest days, our flesh will pull hard toward self-gratification, apathy, laziness, pleasure. All the more on the hard days. Everyday faithfulness requires vigilance. It takes discipline and cultivates patience. It requires a long-term plan because it requires commitment to a long view of sanctification. There will be no instant gains. But there will be joy and growth as daily perseverance yields a life of faithfulness to Jesus.

Each day that we persevere will bring us closer to the mind of Christ, nearer to reflecting his image. Even when we feel we've failed (because we will), when holding on to the truth in a hostile culture feels too hard, when we're spread too thin, when we wonder if steadfastness matters when no one is looking, we can still get up in the morning knowing that new mercies abound from the God who works in us as we press forward in everyday faithfulness. Our confidence is rooted in God's faithfulness, and our obedience is fed by Christ's example of it.

I don't want you to take this book as a call to "do more" or "be better." This is not a book about walking a straight line of discipline to earn God's favor. Because of Jesus's work at the cross, you already have his favor. Christ's righteousness has been credited to your account, there is no more condemnation for you, and you can rest securely in God's love for you (Rom. 8:1, 38–39). Instead, I want to encourage you through the following chapters to build habits into your life that will aid you in knowing and enjoying Christ *now* so you'll still be

---

2. D. A. Carson, *For the Love of God, Vol. 2: A Daily Companion for Discovering the Riches of God's Word* (Wheaton, IL: Crossway, 2006), 23.

knowing and enjoying him long after you put this book down. Growth doesn't come from rigidly following rules. Rather, it is a gift that God gives to those who have truly tasted his goodness (see 1 Pet. 2:2–3). In building your life around tasting his goodness, you'll be equipped to enjoy him no matter what demands and pressures of life press against your faith. With God's help, we'll follow him more tomorrow than we did today. This is everyday faithfulness.

Faithful Like Margaret

Margaret was born in 1927 and was saved at the age of ten when the church across the street from her one-room schoolhouse offered revival services after school. After hearing the gospel at one of those services, Margaret repented of her sins and believed in Christ. With little access to discipleship, Margaret struggled to grow in her faith until she was connected to a church family as a young adult.

Margaret married, adopted a son after years of infertility, and then had a daughter. She grew in her faith in Christ as she learned to treasure the Bible, value church attendance, and commit to both personal prayer and times of prayer with various prayer partners over the years.

Though she has spent many of her adult years widowed and living alone, Margaret's life has been built around studying the Bible and sharing it with anyone who enters her home—whether that's a neighbor, a relative, or a repairman. Her passion for speaking of Christ is an overflow of a life submerged in the practices of everyday faithfulness. Decades of prayer and Bible study prepared her for trials late in life when she struggled with vision problems. As her vision waned, she worried about being unable to read her Bible. Yet all the years of nourishing her soul with the word meant that the scriptures were stored in her heart and mind.

Anyone who knows Margaret knows that she is committed to prayer every morning. Claiming the access she's been given to the Father through Jesus, Margaret often remarks that she delights in "taking hold of the horns of the altar" when interceding for others. She has lived many long years in quiet faithfulness to Christ because his word, his church, and his presence have sustained her through every one.

2

Faithful When You're Just Not Disciplined

When my husband and I were in our early twenties, we decided to run a half marathon. It seemed reasonable to us that two couch potatoes could become runners during the twelve weeks of training, but that was an assumption built on the idea that we would actually complete all of the training. In truth, we completed less than half of it. (What can I say? It was 2006, and we had just discovered Netflix.) The race was a disaster. We dealt with muscle cramps, knee pain, low blood sugar, stomach problems, and more. My toes were bleeding by the time we limped across the finish line, and my husband promised he would never agree to such madness again.

Runners *run*. They don't hope one day they'll wake up and feel like running. They run when they feel like it, and more importantly, when they don't. Anything we want to learn and grow in doesn't happen in one big decision but in thousands of little ones. I could have been a marathon runner if I'd made the everyday decisions to run and train on all the days between sign-up day and race day. It wasn't enough to sign up for the race and hope I'd eventually drift toward athleticism.

We have similar expectations about our spiritual health sometimes, don't we? I've found it to be a common sentiment among harried, busy Christians that the next season of life will find them more disciplined, more faithful, more devoted to Christ simply because they'll be older and wiser with the passage of time. If only they can just get through these next few hectic years on a string of emergency prayers and a smattering of verse-of-the-day emails! I've had those expectations, and I'll be the first to tell you it simply doesn't work that way. Stumbling across the finish line with bloody feet taught me the value of daily investment for a desired outcome. Our perseverance in spiritual growth requires daily decisions of investment, and the good news is that God has given us everything we need.

In this chapter, we'll discuss the gifts of Scripture, prayer, and the church as the God-ordained means for nourishing our souls. We'll learn to distinguish legalism from laziness and why neither should keep us from drawing near to the Lord each day. We'll look at some practical ways to employ the gifts God has given us for holding fast to the gospel for those of us—including me!—who struggle to implement the vital practice of spiritual disciplines.

Everything We Need for Life and Godliness

Knowing that God has promised to complete the work he began in us, we are well equipped to practice perseverance, as Peter explains in his second epistle:

> His divine power has granted to us all things that pertain to life and godliness, through the knowledge of him, who called us to his own glory and excellence, by which he has

granted to us his precious and very great promises, so that through them you may become partakers of the divine nature, having escaped from the corruption that is in the world because of sinful desire. For this very reason, make every effort to supplement your faith with virtue, and virtue with knowledge, and knowledge with self-control, and self-control with steadfastness, and steadfastness with godliness, and godliness with brotherly affection, and brotherly affection with love. (2 Pet. 1:3–7)

Because God has given us his "precious and very great promises," Peter encourages believers to supplement faith with godliness, knowledge, steadfastness, and self-control—all of which have a direct impact on our relationships with other believers. He underscores his exhortation with a warning:

For if these qualities are yours and are increasing, they keep you from being ineffective or unfruitful in the knowledge of our Lord Jesus Christ. For whoever lacks these qualities is so nearsighted that he is blind, having forgotten that he was cleansed from his former sins. Therefore, brothers, be all the more diligent to confirm your calling and election, for if you practice these qualities you will never fall. For in this way there will be richly provided for you an entrance into the eternal kingdom of our Lord and Savior Jesus Christ. (2 Pet. 1:8–11)

If you are making every effort to grow in knowledge of Christ and in godliness, then you are bearing the fruit of true faith in him, and you will "never fall." However, if you are *not* eager to diligently "confirm your calling," then you may be blind to your true spiritual condition. While many of us endure seasons of spiritual dryness (more on this in chap. 7), the long-term patterns of neglect should give us pause about our spiritual condition. If we spend much of our lives resistant to pursuing godliness in the ways God has given us, then we might be deceiving ourselves as to whether we have been cleansed from our sins through Christ. If we have been cleansed, then we should long to become like the one who did the cleansing! The power of God within us aids us in our endeavors to grow in godliness, and through the habits of grace we can supplement our faith, building it up with effectiveness and fruitfulness.

With the help and investment of God, the path to spiritual maturity and growth begins and travels through the pages of Scripture and prayer, both individually and within the community of faith. The apostle Paul said that every word of Scripture is breathed out by God, divinely inspired by him and without error. His word is wisdom unto salvation, and after that, for sanctification (see 2 Tim. 3:16). To follow Jesus on day one, look to him in the word. To follow Jesus on day 9,412, look to him in the word. The words of the Lord are for both our salvation and our sanctification.

In his book on spiritual disciplines, Donald Whitney says, "We find in Scripture how to live in a way that is pleasing to God as well as best and most fulfilling for ourselves. None of this eternally essential information can be found anywhere else except the Bible. Therefore if we would know God and be godly, we must know the Word of God—intimately."[1] And Paul tells us godliness comes by being trained in God's word:

> If you put these [teachings] before the brothers, you will be
> a good servant of Christ Jesus, being trained in the words
> of the faith and of the good doctrine that you have fol-
> lowed. Have nothing to do with irreverent, silly myths.

---

1. Donald S. Whitney, *Spiritual Disciplines for the Christian Life* (Colorado Springs, CO: NavPress, 1991), 28.

Rather train yourself for godliness; for while bodily training is of some value, godliness is of value in every way, as
it holds promise for the present life and also for the life to
come. (1 Tim. 4:6–8)

Do you see how faithfulness is tied to godliness? And how
godliness is tied to God's word? Being trained by the words
and good doctrine of the Lord requires being rooted in those
words and doctrine. The resulting benefits aren't just for this
life but for the one to come. Discipline for the purpose of godliness keeps us faithful on all the days between the first day of
following Christ and the day we see him face-to-face, ensuring
us that we *will* see him face-to-face. Those are very long-term
benefits! Christ's finished work on the cross is sure, but our
perseverance in knowing God through his word and prayer
reveals and refines our genuine faith.

Jesus Gives Us Access

Throughout this book, we'll return to the habits of Bible reading, prayer, and corporate worship as the gifts God has given
us to remain faithful to him. These spiritual disciplines help to
keep us on the path of spiritual maturity, of growth in Christ,
of looking more and more like him every day. God ordained
that the path of sanctification be paved with Scripture and
prayer, and we must submit ourselves to his plan for our spiritual maturity. The writer of Hebrews encourages us to hold
fast to the access we've been given to God through Jesus at
the cross:

Therefore, brothers, since we have confidence to enter the
holy places by the blood of Jesus, by the new and living way
that he opened for us through the curtain, that is, through
his flesh, and since we have a great priest over the house

of God, *let us draw near* with a true heart in full assurance of faith, with our hearts sprinkled clean from an evil conscience and our bodies washed with pure water. *Let us hold fast the confession* of our hope without wavering, for he who promised is faithful. And *let us consider how to stir up one another* to love and good works, not neglecting to meet together, as is the habit of some, but encouraging one another, and all the more as you see the Day drawing near. (Heb. 10:19–25)

In light of this amazing free access to the Father, we're charged to do three things: (1) draw near, (2) hold fast to the confession, and (3) stir up fellow believers to love and good deeds. We can obey through our individual and corporate spiritual disciplines.

First, we draw near to God. I can think of no better way to draw near to God than through prayer. Tim Keller says that prayer is "the way we know God, the way we finally treat God *as* God. Prayer is simply the key to everything we need to do and be in life."[2] Prayer gives us the opportunity to enjoy God's presence and talk with him. We can confess our sins, repent, and pour out our concerns and needs to him. We can trust God with all we've heaped upon his capable shoulders. Devotion to prayer is fruit of a life that has been changed by the power of the gospel of Christ.

Second, we hold fast to our confession of hope. How can we hold on to what we believe in if we do not make a regular study of what we believe? Our hearts are easily desensitized by our culture, our entertainment choices, our desires for comfort. We can unknowingly lean toward unbiblical but popular theology if we are not reorienting ourselves to the truths of Scrip-

2. Timothy Keller, *Prayer: Experiencing Awe and Intimacy with God* (New York: Penguin, 2014), 18.

ture on a regular basis. We hold fast to our confession through regular exposure to God's word. Bank tellers can quickly detect a counterfeit bill because they've made a careful study of the authentic form. Similarly, we can detect counterfeit confessions of faith when we're anchored to the authentic gospel.

Third, we encourage other believers by meeting together regularly. Stirring one another up to love and good deeds must be done in community. If we neglect corporate worship, we miss the opportunity to encourage and be encouraged in our confession of hope. We cannot obey all the "one another" passages of Scripture if we are not meeting regularly with our fellow believers. The local church is God's gift to us to help us grow in godliness, remain faithful to him, and hold fast to the gospel. Through accountability, fellowship, confession, worship, and hearing the proclamation of God's word together, we will be more likely to remain steadfast in our individual disciplines of prayer and Bible reading. The church keeps us from wandering away in sin, helps us carry our burdens, provides teaching through the word, and gives oversight for our souls. You need the church and the church needs you!

Legalism or Laziness

For every article or book you read praising the practice of spiritual disciplines, you'll find another decrying a regimented spiritual life for fear of legalism. It's true that legalism—thinking we can attain a righteous standing before God by our own works—is possible at any point in a Christian's life. Our enemy the devil is always looking for ways to deceive us, so even the good things in our life are candidates for his perversion. He would like for us to believe that we must *do more* and *be more* in order for God to love us. Think of how "religious" the Pharisees were when their hearts were spiritually bankrupt!

Anything we do in obedience to God we could certainly do with wrong motives—to feel superior to others, to keep a nicely checked column of boxes to display our holiness, to prove to ourselves that God didn't waste his grace on us, to try to continue in the flesh what the Holy Spirit has begun (see Gal. 3:3).[3] If we're reading our Bibles daily so that we have a page of perfectly checked boxes on our yearly reading plan, then we are missing the point. If we flaunt that perfectly checked plan to others, then we have received our full reward in that moment of pride. If we read our Bibles hoping God will love us more, then we've forgotten that he loved us while we were yet sinners and sent Jesus to die for us. Legalism is a real concern, but we address it by regularly examining our motives. Are we seeking the Lord in his word to be loved by him or because we already are? The answer to that question matters.

I understand the fear that building habits might make us prideful, but I've found that the fear of legalism is rarely the real reason for prayerlessness or a lack of commitment to regular Bible reading. Nor is it the reason for poor attendance at church. Usually, we neglect our habits of grace from plain old laziness.

Those years when I repeatedly confessed spiritual negligence to my accountability partner (which ironically coincided with that half marathon fiasco) were not a result of legalism but of laziness. I knew God wanted me to read my Bible and pray. I could list many reasons why I resisted: I was busy, I had a job, I was tired, I was "training" for a half marathon. But the truth is, I was lazy. I didn't want to do the work of study. I would rather read fiction than the Bible, sleep than

---

3. Christine Hoover has written a helpful book about depending on God's grace after salvation rather than good works: *From Good to Grace: Letting Go of the Goodness Gospel* (Grand Rapids, MI: Baker, 2015).

pray, and watch my favorite show than memorize Scripture. I wanted to be faithful to Christ, but I didn't want to follow his path to get there. My laziness revealed a refusal to submit to God's design for growth.

My resistance to exercising the spiritual disciplines was also fed by my misunderstanding of spiritual growth. I wanted instant gains for minimal efforts. I didn't want to put down slow-growing roots; I wanted to be a chia pet. I wanted to add water and see growth immediately. But think about the stability of something that grows overnight. How deep are those roots? We can't live as chia seed sprouts! We need long, sustained growth that is strong enough to uphold us when trials come, that's sturdy enough to withstand illness or busy seasons or broken relationships. And that takes time.

A couple of spurts of Bible reading, prayer, and church involvement are certainly better than none, but real fruit can't grow on a loosely anchored vine. Jesus was clear that life and growth come only from abiding in him: "Abide in me, and I in you. As the branch cannot bear fruit by itself, unless it abides in the vine, neither can you, unless you abide in me" (John 15:4). Earlier, Jesus says that loving him means obeying his commands (John 14:15). As you and I stand on this side of the gospel story, we have an entire book of those commands. We can demonstrate our love for God by our obedience because he first loved us.

Practicing spiritual disciplines may feel like work at first. Establishing new habits always presses against our apathy in uncomfortable ways. But one day your heart will catch up to the regimen. One day you'll look back and see growth. And one day, you'll find great joy in these daily expressions of faith. You'll discover that the benefits of being rooted in God's word reach deep and wide.

Rooted by a River

The practice of reading and meditating on the word of God is nearly as old as the written word itself. When God gave the law to Moses, he commanded the people to keep his words before them at all times, to talk of the law often, to teach it to their children, to think of it morning and night (Deut. 6:4–9). God's people loved God with heart, soul, and mind by keeping his words wrapped around their every waking thought. Reciting the words of his law helped the people remember who God is, what God had done for them, and how to live as his people.

We have so much more than the Israelites did! We have the fully revealed gospel story. We can read Genesis through Malachi with an eye on Jesus. We have eyewitness accounts of Jesus's life, death, and resurrection. We have the beginnings of his kingdom, the early church, and the promises about his return. God's word is a true feast!

Psalm 1 is a helpful analogy for what treasuring the word of God looks like—the practice, the purpose, and the benefits. We're introduced to the happy or blessed man who avoids sin by delighting in the word of God. He meditates on it daily (and nightly). The psalm compares him to a tree that's planted by a river. When the roots of a tree feed off a continuous stream of water, the tree receives sustaining nourishment no matter the season or scarcity of rain. It's not a difficult metaphor to decipher. If we are sustained by God's word, we'll be nourished in every season no matter the obstacles to growth that we encounter.

But that's not all the tree does. The tree bears fruit, and the man who feeds his faithfulness with the goodness of God's word prospers in all he does (Ps. 1:3). But think about bearing fruit for a moment. Does a tree pick its own fruit? Does it enjoy the bounty that grows from steady nourishment? No, the fruit is for the benefit of others. And here's where the analogy between the tree and the man who loves the Bible really reaches beyond our own personal benefits. When we are equipped by God's word for every good work, the other people in our life get to enjoy the fruit.

The people in your church need you to be devoted to the word and to prayer. Our spiritual disciplines don't just benefit us. We don't follow Jesus in isolation. Our growth and our perseverance also encourage growth and perseverance in our brothers and sisters in Christ. When we are suffering or living through a dry season, the perseverance of other believers who invest in our spiritual well-being helps us. We do the same for others when they struggle. Developing a habit of prayer provides a way for us to keep our promise to intercede for others who are hurting. Regular Bible intake strengthens our faith so we can help a friend who is fighting doubt or temptation. Your faithfulness to hold fast to Christ will encourage the members of your church to do likewise.

The effects reach beyond the doors of our church buildings, too. As we study God's word and pray regularly for unbelievers, we'll find that the words of the Lord are readily on our lips. When the truth of the gospel is firmly entrenched in our minds, we'll look for opportunities to share Christ with them.

Both the church and the world need you to be faithful in your spiritual disciplines. As Christians we depend upon one another—to uphold one another when we're weak or discouraged. And the world needs the hope of the gospel that we experience every single day.

Practically Speaking

Perhaps you recognize in yourself a desire to be faithful in spiritual disciplines but don't know where to begin. The good news is that, as my friend advised me so many years ago, you can begin walking the path of perseverance today! Remember, God is invested in your spiritual maturity and has given you what you need to grow. As you begin to practice prayer and Bible reading, expect it to feel difficult for a while. On the days you forget or oversleep, don't get discouraged or believe the lie that God loves you less. You aren't practicing spiritual disciplines so God will love you more. You're practicing them because he already loves you and has cleansed you from your sins.

The best place to begin is with a plan. With a plan in place, you've taken all future decision-making out of the equation. You won't have to redecide each day how you're going to practice Bible reading or prayer. Make the decision now so all you have to do tomorrow is show up. First, pick a place. Put your Bible, notebooks, and pens in a place where you can regularly sit. Next, pick a time. The time you choose will depend on your particular schedule and commitments, but most find that morning is best. Then, pick a plan (I'll give you some suggestions) and follow it. Finally, tell someone. Accountability is a gift when it comes to developing new habits. Have a friend or mentor from church call or text regularly to ask how you're doing.

Now, for the plan. A daily Bible reading plan builds some additional accountability into your life. You don't have to wait until January 1 to start a plan. A year can begin on the date of your choosing. It's helpful to use a plan that keeps you in multiple parts of the Bible at once.[4] You're less likely to get bogged down in a challenging book like Leviticus when you're also reading Psalms, Proverbs, and Colossians. Daily reading, as uncomplicated as it sounds, can change your life. Simple,

---

4. A one-year Bible reading plan can be found at https://static.crossway.org/excerpt/esv-mcheyne-reading-plan.pdf.

daily absorption of the words of the Lord is the kind of nourishment your soul thrives on.

Another method of study is to walk through one book of the Bible at a time while answering some basic questions about the text. Answering the questions below helps me to read the Bible with God in mind, to look at all of Scripture through a gospel lens, and to arrive at appropriate application. Making summary statements helps me articulate what the passage says, giving me an easy way to speak the words of the Lord to my friends at church for encouragement and to move a conversation with my unbelieving friends to spiritual things.

Below are my simple steps that you can follow for your Bible reading; I've included symbols to help you remember them.[5] Read the text several times and establish the background (study Bibles are helpful for this). Then move through the following steps:

▲ Make a general summary statement about the text.
† What does this teach me about God?
↓ What does this teach me about man?
† What does this text teach me about Christ? (Or, how does this text point me to Christ?)
✓ How can I apply this text to my life?
▲ Make a second general summary statement about the text.

Using these steps, you can work through one book of the Bible over the course of a month or a year—you choose. Read a chapter a day and answer each question. Or, stretch out the process over a week, reading the same chapter each day and tackling one step per day. When you're reading the Bible and

---

5. This is just one way to study the Scriptures. If you have other methods you're familiar with, use those. If you've never attempted Bible study by yourself, a helpful resource is Jen Wilkin's *Women of the Word: How to Study the Bible with Both Our Hearts and Our Minds* (Wheaton, IL: Crossway, 2014).

thinking through what you learn, you're like a tree planted by a stream, always nourished, always bearing fruit. Work through this process with a friend or small study group and discuss what you've learned each week. You'll learn more in community, and you'll be more likely to stay with the plan.

Praying through the passages you've read and studied can further plant the truth into your heart. Praying through the text I'm studying helps me memorize and meditate on it. And speaking the words of the psalms to the Lord often gives me the language of lament or praise that I struggle to come up with myself. Praying Paul's prayers for the church in Philippians 1 or Ephesians 3 aids in my prayers for my church.

My pastor-husband has long encouraged our congregation to pray with a list, and I've found it helpful in organizing my thoughts and fighting distractions. I start inward, beginning with my own sanctification, and move outward to my husband, my children, my church, my friends and extended family, unbelieving friends and acquaintances, missionaries and church planters, and the persecuted church around the world. The list keeps me focused and guarantees that I will intercede for the people I've promised to pray for.

Maybe, like me, you've never successfully trained for a marathon. Maybe you hit snooze at six o'clock in the morning too many times or choose Netflix over a good night's sleep. Maybe getting to the gym regularly is about as likely as choosing salad over a cheeseburger. Maybe you've struggled, as I have, to make a regular practice of the spiritual disciplines God has given us to know and make him known. Yet the benefits of rooting ourselves in his word, in prayer, and in corporate worship reach far beyond what any diet or exercise plan ever could. If we want to be equipped to encourage believers and share the gospel with unbelievers, we must hold fast to our confession of hope regularly. If we want to grow in our awareness of God's promises, we must draw near to him. We must train our hearts to default to Scripture now so that when life is unbearably hard, we'll turn to our Lord out of a long-practiced habit. Perseverance now feeds our faithfulness later and sustains us for future trials.

Faithful Like Dorothy

Dorothy grew up one of twelve children in rural Tennessee. After she married and began raising two daughters, she worked the graveyard shift for twenty-five years as a telephone operator.

After retirement, Dorothy struggled to keep a normal schedule, but she ordered her life around prayer and Bible study to grow in her knowledge of the God who loved and saved her. Whatever was on the docket for her day came after she spent her first waking hours (whenever they might be) in a quiet room with the door shut where she knelt before a bench with her Bible fanned open.

As a result of her devotion to the Lord, Dorothy was deeply steeped in his word, blessed with wisdom, kindness, generosity, joy, and even peace when her husband died suddenly from an aneurism. Her steadfastness continued throughout the next decade as she deteriorated in the grip of disease.

Dorothy's prayers, wisdom, teaching, and love benefited innumerable individuals in her community and church. The long line of people at Dorothy's funeral spoke of her faithfulness to Jesus and stood as evidence of her years of prayer and love for his word. Like a tree planted by a river that bore fruit in every season, Dorothy's life bore fruit for the benefit of others, glorifying God with her steadfast faithfulness. She was faithful because she knew he was first faithful to her.

3

Faithful When Your Hands Are Full

Several years ago, when I was parenting an infant and a second grader, I had a day that was so challenging, I still use it as a standard for how well or poorly things are going in life. My husband had been tied up in meetings all day followed by an emergency pastoral visit during the evening. I was dealing with some health problems in addition to the ins and outs of an unusually busy day of work and parenting. After a hectic morning of school drop-off, grocery shopping, errands, and housework, I found myself trying to comfort a teething baby and keep my older son entertained while I taught an afternoon of piano lessons. Teaching scales and dominant seventh chord inversions for three hours while soothing a feverish baby wasn't easy! Later, I prepped and served dinner, washed dishes, and tidied up the house. I faced four loads of laundry, confusing math homework, bottle feedings, and diapers. I gave baths and did bedtime routines and tried to love on my kids who'd had to put up with a harried and crabby mom all day. After my kids were asleep, I collapsed on the couch, glanced at my forgotten Bible on the coffee table, and wondered if I'd ever feel like picking it up again.

When your hands are full and your time doesn't seem to belong to you, how in the world do you hold on to spiritual disciplines? Should we even worry about pursuing faithfulness during seasons when work and caregiving are top priorities? The cumulative effect of lost sleep, cleaning up messes, and chauffeuring children to school or extracurriculars can wear us down quickly. And what about the later years when you think you're done caring for family members but find that your elderly parents need you as much as your babies did?

Whether you're caring for a houseful of babies and toddlers, working through the drama of the teen years, or caring for an aging parent, seasons of caregiving come with a unique kind of exhaustion. We try to wrap our heads around the number of years we'll be in this season and figure we have to move anything else important to the back burner until the end is in sight. Even spiritual disciplines. Who can read the Bible when the baby is crying, right?

While there will be times you have to set down your Bible to pick up a crying child or tend to an emotional preteen, pushing aside your spiritual disciplines until later in life will not aid you in remaining faithful until then. Many of us will likely be living in caregiving seasons for many years. To forego the habits of prayer, Bible reading, and church involvement until life is less chaotic will mean that a significant portion of our lives is spent largely without attachment to and dependency upon Christ. And one could argue these are the years we need him the most!

Consider this: if you have three children two years apart in age, then you will likely have children in your home for at least twenty-four years. That's more than a quarter of the average life span for women in North America, and nearly half of your adulthood![1] We can't afford to put off our spiritual growth for two decades. One seasoned mother said, "I was pretty immature as a Christian and as a young mom. I have regrets over not pursuing Christ as much as I should have. . . . I wish someone would have told me. The young years matter."[2]

When we're caring for children or aging parents (or for some of us, both at the same time), we must ask ourselves: How can we hold fast to the Lord through his word, prayer, and his church? I want to encourage you that it's not only possible to press on in perseverance, it's *necessary*.

Christians Survive Differently

I well remember the exhaustion of brand-new motherhood. When my first son was born, I didn't pick up my Bible for months. I was so sure that I'd arrive at the magical land of discipline later when my baby wasn't so needy. I didn't realize that keeping the habits of Bible reading and prayer when it was difficult to do so would have laid the path to Bible reading and prayer later when it wasn't so hard. When the days of chaos eased up, I found myself uninspired to practice any kind of spiritual discipline. The indifference I had excused as survival mode became my normal way of life, and my days were devoid of any regular connection to Christ outside of church attendance.

I've heard the "survival mode" rationalization many times from other Christians, too. *I'm too busy. My time is not my own. I was up with the baby all night. I haven't slept in weeks. I'm just trying to survive right now.* Oh, these are hard seasons, friend!

---

1. "Life Expectancy in North America," Statista website, accessed June 15, 2019, https://www.statista.com/statistics/274513/life-expectancy-in-north-america/.

2. Noelle Lamb, Google submission form to author, February 1, 2019.

The exhaustion is real. Just surviving feels like the right answer sometimes, doesn't it? Yet what I've learned from older, more seasoned believers is that knowing Christ is the only way to endure those tough years when you're pulled in a thousand different directions. If we're not holding on to him now, how can we be sure we'll be holding on to him later?

As believers, we live differently from the unbelieving world around us. We are new creatures in Christ, and everything we do is to be done by, through, and for him (see Col. 1:15–17). Survival mode for the weary Christian is not hibernation *from* Christ but perseverance *in* Christ. The things we tend to shuffle to the bottom of the to-do list are the very gifts God has given us to keep us near his side. We can't survive disconnected from him. Prioritizing his word, prayer, and fellowship with our church is what helps us survive! Perhaps those habits will look a bit different during the hardest seasons of caregiving, but pushing spiritual disciplines aside until life settles down is not what will help us persevere through tough days. We persevere to the end by persevering to the end of *this* day.

When your reserves feel empty, when your patience is thin, when you can barely stay awake, saturating yourself with Scripture *is* survival. When the baby won't sleep, when your responsibilities at work keep you up at night, when your parent with Alzheimer's can't remember you, when the laundry of four under four never ends, prayer *is* survival. When you are too weary to sing praises to the Lord, when you're wrestling a rowdy bunch during the sermon, when it's all you can do just to sit upright in the pew, being present with your church family *is* survival. These expressions of faithfulness to Christ are the means by which he keeps you faithful, even if they're less structured during the chaotic years of caregiving. Survival mode for the Christian whose hands are full must include the things that help her soul survive.

True Rest When You're Always Needed

Caregiving requires deep reserves of self-sacrifice. The loss of sleep, of personal pursuits, time, finances, and more makes life feel like a sieve. Everything that's poured in is immediately poured out for the people we take care of. In putting the needs of others before our own, we pattern our lives after Jesus. He is our example in all things, but we see his selflessness especially in the ways he loved people, served his disciples, and died in our place for our sins. He traveled and taught as a poor, itinerant preacher with no home, no wife or children, and no possessions. The sick sought him out everywhere, the crowds pressed in constantly. Jesus knew what it was to be surrounded by the neediness of others.

How did Jesus handle being in constant demand? First, he intentionally sought out times alone to pray to his Father. Second, he rested. In Mark 6, the disciples returned to Jesus after they had gone out teaching his message. Jesus, too, had been busy teaching and healing the sick. His invitation to the disciples to "come away by yourselves to a desolate place and rest a while," came on the heels of a period so busy they'd not even had time to eat a proper meal (Mark 6:30–32). A few chapters prior, Jesus slipped away very early in the morning to pray in a desolate place (Mark 1:35). He'd just spent days healing the ill and demon-possessed, one right after the other. In Mark 4, Jesus fell asleep on a boat during a storm at the end of a long day of teaching. Jesus didn't shrug off his responsibilities of teaching and healing, but neither did he put off the things that he needed physically and spiritually to continue in his work. He sought time with the Father, and he sought rest. If Jesus the Son of God needed the rhythms of rest and prayer, how much more do we?

Jesus gives us a pattern to emulate, but he also tells us the best way to rest when we are weary in body and soul. More than we need actual physical rest (though we do need that), we need rest for our souls that is found only in him. Jesus said, "Come to me, all who labor and are heavy laden, and I will give you rest. Take my yoke upon you, and learn from me, for I am gentle and lowly in heart, and you will find rest for your souls. For my yoke is easy, and my burden is light" (Matt. 11:28–30). What we don't see in this passage is permission to disconnect from prayer and Jesus's words just because we're weighed down by burdens. Jesus doesn't say, "If you're weary, ignore what I'm saying and wait until you're not so burdened." He doesn't say, "Come to me later, when you're not weary." He tells the weary to come to him, take up his yoke, learn from him, and find rest.

Gloria Furman writes, "If I don't renew my mind through the truths of God's Word, then the fog doesn't burn off and let the light of gospel hope shine in. By the end of the day I am lost in a cloud of discouragement that doesn't lift. We need the compass of eternity to direct our perspective."[3] The way we come to God and learn from him is to take up our Bibles and know him through his word. The way we find rest is in seeking the Lord in prayer. We do this on our own and also when we hear the proclamation of the word and examine our hearts during communion with fellow believers in corporate worship together. His yoke is lighter and easier than legalistic rules and false religion, but it doesn't allow us to roam free from all connection to him. His yoke tethers us to him and pulls us in the direction he leads us. We won't find rest for our souls in loosening that tether from Christ. We find rest in staying by

3. Gloria Furman, *Treasuring Christ When Your Hands Are Full: Gospel Meditations for Busy Moms* (Wheaton, IL: Crossway, 2014), 52.

his side no matter how busy and exhausting our days might be. *Christ* is our survival mode.

As you serve and care for others, remember that Jesus knew what it was like to be needed. Emulate him by making time for prayer and the words of the Lord. You'll be equipped to persevere when you are tethered to him. As you read his word, you'll gain confidence in his love. As you pray, you'll experience his fellowship and his help. As you unite with Christ's body in your local church, you'll receive encouragement and support. Here's some good news for you, weary friend: Christ is at work in you as you persevere during these challenging days of busyness. As you pattern your life after Jesus's—even when it feels like you've nothing left to give—the Holy Spirit is living in you and helping you persevere. He will use your habits of prayer and Bible reading to reveal your sin, to remind you of Jesus's sacrifice for you on the cross, to lead you in obedience to him. Physical rest is important. But the rest that Jesus offers nourishes our souls so that we can continue living for him—even with a long to-do list.

As you press forward with regular faithfulness amidst a mountain of laundry, a rotation of diaper changes and nighttime feedings, or basic acts of care for an aging parent, the Lord sees you. He knows you are weary, and he is working good from it. He has compassion on you when you struggle to pick up your Bible or sleep through prayer. Christ is your example, but he is also your helper as he intercedes for you to keep following him in faithfulness (Rom. 8:34).

Show Others Where Your Treasure Is

In addition to nourishing our own souls, daily perseverance blesses those around us. When you determine to follow Jesus tomorrow more than you did today, you are showing the ones in your home, your office, your neighborhood, and your circle of friends that Jesus is worth every ounce of regular, ordinary spectacular faithfulness. Believe me, they are watching.

Growing up, I was an early riser. Every morning, I would stumble out of bed and head to the kitchen to find my mother sitting at the table with her Bible and notebook fanned out in front of her. She always greeted me with a smile and a hug but then went back to her studying. I knew from a young age that my mother treasured the Lord because she never gave up her habit of meeting with him in the mornings. Whether she realized it or not, my mother was showing me where her life's greatest treasure was found: in Jesus. She was also showing me that followers of Jesus follow him by knowing him through his word and by praying to him. Regularly. Daily.

The people in your everyday life are watching you as I watched my mother. Her mornings at the kitchen table are as much a part of my childhood as school lunches, Saturday morning cartoons, backyard swing sets, and family dinners. She faithfully followed Christ every day, and I watched her.

This is what I remember when my four-year-old wanders into the living room with bedhead and a sleepy smile at five thirty in the morning. It is good for him to watch his mother follow Jesus. Sometimes I invite him onto the couch with me where he pages through his picture Bible while I finish praying or reading. Yes, it's inconvenient. Yes, it's distracting. Yes, it's an interruption to my only quiet hour of the entire day. But we parents need to invite our children to see the tangible ways we are learning to treasure Christ.

The way you follow Jesus will influence the way your children follow him. Look at yourself through the eyes of your children and ask yourself if they know who you treasure.

Based on the way you've prioritized your days, will they know your treasure is Jesus?

Practically Speaking

You may have picked up this book for this very section of this very chapter. How can you hold on to the spiritual disciplines that feed your faithfulness when your hands are more than full? How do you freely confess your failure to treasure Christ while not giving yourself a free pass to disconnect from him? What steps can you implement that will encourage you to follow Jesus in this very challenging season? To answer these questions, I am drawing from the wisdom of others who have loved Jesus better and longer than I have.

One seasoned Christian mom told me that she always felt like she was either "passing or failing" when it came to spiritual disciplines during her years of child-raising and working two jobs. She would agree with me that we need to eliminate those two words from our vocabulary. Many of us teeter to one side or the other: guilt for not being as faithful as we'd like to be or giving ourselves a free pass because this is just where we are in life. I'd like to offer Paul's encouragement here. We're not perfect, and we won't be this side of heaven. But that shouldn't discourage us from pressing on in perseverance. Instead, let's "[forget] what lies behind and [strain] foward to what lies ahead," and let's "press on toward the goal for the prize of the upward call of God in Christ Jesus" (Phil. 3:13–14).

Spiritual maturity recognizes the need to persevere in spite of past failings. Whatever yesterday looked like, start over fresh tomorrow. Jesus isn't standing with his arms crossed and a disapproving glare. He loves you, and he paid the penalty for your sins on the cross. When you make time with him a priority, you will be more and more certain of his love for you, even on the days you can't seem to show up. You'll see your sin more readily, you'll grasp his grace more acutely, you'll remember his promises to sanctify you, and you'll know with certainty that one day you'll be with him forever, when nothing will deter or distract you from his glory.

Committing to spiritual disciplines may look different during busy seasons, but you can still hold on to God's word, prayer, and the church. Make your plan, as I mentioned in the last chapter. You'll have to be flexible with children or family members who need you, but you can plan for more regularity if you choose to get up a little earlier or spend the last half hour before bed with the Lord. Denying yourself, taking up your cross, and following Jesus might look like sacrificing an extra hour of sleep or turning off Netflix an hour earlier than usual. Your faithfulness to Christ *will* you cost you something. Oh, but the benefits are eternal and beyond comparison! Drawing near to God through his word and through prayer will transcend and transform your busy day like nothing else. When you're facing a mountain of laundry, your mind will be filled with God's promises. When the nap schedule is interrupted for the fifth time today, you'll remember the warnings against sin and guard yourself from anger. When your elderly parents ask the same questions again and again, you'll have comforting words of Scripture ready to offer them.

Scripture memorization is another helpful tool to further engage with the Bible. You can use note cards or an app like Verses or The Bible Memory App to work through a passage of Scripture, memorizing one phrase at a time. As you read, work through the study questions I mentioned in the last chapter. What does this verse teach me about God? About man? How does it make me think about Jesus? What can I apply from this verse to my life? This is a simple way to saturate your heart with the truths of God's word. One trick we use in our home is to print out a text for memorization, slide it upside down into a gallon-sized Ziploc bag, and then tape the bag (seal side down) to the wall of the shower. Every time you're in the shower, you can work on memorization.

One other technological gift to utilize when you're feeling desperate for time with the Lord is to listen to the Bible through an audio app. Exposure to the word can and should happen in many forms. To really meditate on a passage, listen to it several times. This will also aid in memorization. One mother of grown sons recommends singing the scriptures to your children.[4] Not only will you be singing the powerful words of the Lord over your children, which can aid you in praying for them, but you'll also be memorizing Scripture with them as you sing. Seeds Family Worship and the New City Catechism songs are two great resources for singing God's truth with and for your children. These might also be helpful tools to use with your older parents who get confused and can't read or study the word anymore.

You're probably already praying a lot of emergency prayers throughout your busiest days, and that's a good thing! We can't persevere through hectic work and family schedules without the Lord's help. But during these especially difficult days, your soul will benefit from regular, intentional prayer. Seek windows of time when you can really speak to the Lord and praise him for sustaining you, when you can plead for his help in avoiding the sins of grumbling and complaining, when you can ask him to produce patience in your life. You'll find peace that transcends even the hardest days when you obey the Lord by praying to him.

---

4. Karen Govier, Google form submission to author, February 18, 2019.

When you can, strive for a time that's dedicated solely to the Lord. There is no substitute for laying open the word of God and tethering yourself to Christ through it. Though fatigue is an expected companion to the years of caring for others, try to give your most alert moments to Christ. John Piper says there are many things you can do tired, but studying God's word is exponentially harder when you're sleepy (and you'll be more likely to quit). He encourages us to move the things we *can* do tired (grocery shopping, folding laundry, cleaning bathrooms, etc.) to the edges of our day and giving our most focused time to Christ.[5]

For some, this will mean opening your Bible during naptime instead of attacking the laundry mountain on your bed. Others will need to push entertainment to the periphery of life in favor of a half hour to read and pray before turning out the light. Most of us will need to sacrifice a little physical rest for true spiritual rest. No moment will be wasted. Even if we are interrupted during the hour we planned for solitude with Christ, we can adapt so we don't lose our time in God's word and prayer. Give yourself permission to enjoy a hectic, interrupted, unquiet "quiet time."

Maybe you'll set your children up with a quiet show while you read and pray. Maybe you'll read Scripture and pray during your lunch hour at work. Maybe you'll read the Bible on your phone while you're feeding the baby or sitting in the waiting room at your parent's medical appointment. Maybe you'll pray through your prayer list as you walk or jog through your neighborhood. Your ordinary faithfulness to Jesus, even when your hands are abundantly full, will point others to the one who holds you in *his* hands. As you care for your growing

---

5. John Piper, "I'm Tired and Busy—How Do I Make Time for the Bible?," Desiring God website, January 7, 2019, https://www.desiringgod.org/interviews/im-tired-and -busy-how-do-i-make-time-for-the-bible.

children, you'll be growing, too. As you serve your parents or aging relatives, you'll be served with the nourishment of truth and God's presence.

You're not on your own here, friend. God has given you the church to help you navigate these beautifully challenging seasons. Lean on your church family for support. Make them aware of any needs you have. This might look like asking someone to watch your children for an afternoon every other week so you can pray and read your Bible for a longer time. Or perhaps it's taking advantage of the nursery volunteers so that you can enjoy an uninterrupted hour during the worship service. The church is also a good place to ask for accountability, especially if you lean toward giving yourself that "I'm too busy to pray" pass. Have a friend text you each week to see how you're doing with Bible reading so that you can remember to continue to taste of his goodness.

Relying on the church for help means you have to show up. One of my fellow church members often tells the story of her grandmother's approach to church attendance while raising a child with chronic illness. "You need to attend church today because you don't know how sick you'll be next week." I love the urgency of this advice! This grandmother encouraged attendance when it was challenging because it could be unavoidable to miss later.

Rather than fitting in church when you can, build your family's schedule around the church schedule. Or, come in spite of the schedule! Come with your fussy babies and your cranky kids. Come with a spit-up splattered shirt and a purse full of snacks. Come with your grief that your elderly mother can't remember your name. Come when you're burned out from an extra-long work week. Come whether you've read the Bible this week or not. Come whether you've slept much this week or not. Just come.

It is tempting to give up after a succession of days without reading Scripture or praying. Know that God's mercy abounds every morning, and his grace covers you. Tomorrow is a new day with brand-new mercies. The Lord loves you, he is working toward your spiritual growth, and he is not done sanctifying you. It doesn't matter so much how yesterday looked. Come to him, and he will give you the rest you really need.

Faithful Like Christine

Christine came to faith in Christ at age seventeen. She had never studied the Bible before but was captivated by the beauty and wisdom of the book of Romans after her conversion. She then built her life around studying the Bible so that she could grow in spiritual maturity. She married and had children but continually rose before dawn each morning to pray and study Scripture. She was at church as often as the doors were open and scheduled her children's days around meeting with the body of Christ.

Christine spent her adult years teaching Sunday school classes and Bible studies for women. Though her devotion to Christ through the church, the Bible, and prayer looked different at various points in her life, she kept herself tethered to Christ at all times. She didn't know throughout her years of perseverance that she was preparing herself for a long season of caring for her elderly mother who suffered from a debilitating form of dementia.

Christine was unable to attend church for six years while she cared for her mother around the clock, along with her younger sister's help. She was not ill-equipped, however. The decades of disciplined devotion to God's word and prayer gave Christine a deep well to draw from as she cared for her mother's needs. She worked on memorization when her mother's needs kept her from a quiet hour of solitude. She prayed constantly, especially on the nights when her mother couldn't rest. When she got discouraged, she remembered that God saw her.

After her mother's death, Christine was able to return to regular church attendance and daily quiet hours of prayer and study. Had the habits not long been ingrained in her life, she might not have persevered so faithfully throughout her mother's illness, but the many years she spent holding fast to Christ helped her to remember that he was holding fast to her.

4

Faithful When You're Waiting

I love Amazon Prime. I can't help but feel excited when I click "Order Now" on an item with the "Free 1-Day Shipping" banner stretched across the product photo. I know that when I click the button, in twenty-four hours a person in a uniform will deliver a package to my doorstep, and I'll revel a little in the power of one-day shipping. For a moment, I have control. I enjoy the ability to command my desires to show up on my doorstep within a twenty-four-hour window. I have the brief contentment that comes in satisfying an urge immediately.

And when the order is inexplicably late, I have the patience of a two-year-old.

I once ordered some clothing that was supposed to arrive before I left for a week-long trip. Wanting to pack the new clothes to take with me, I fretted and checked my phone constantly for delivery updates. The order arrived on my doorstep about twenty-four hours after I left town, and I was surprised by how frustrated I felt. I doubted Amazon's efficiency and complained to anyone who would listen about the company's broken promise of guaranteed one-day shipping. I couldn't get my desired item within my hands fast enough, and it unearthed an ugly truth: I actually *do* have the patience of a two-year-old.

Though I can't compare a delayed Amazon order to the deeper, unfulfilled desires I've felt in my life, I've lived with similar surprise at having to wait for *anything*. Whether it's immediate impatience or the slow-burning version, both reveal an unwillingness to wait well. Unfulfilled desires can unearth a lack of trust in God's sufficiency for us, and sometimes I think that is precisely why God draws us into seasons of waiting. Pastor Zack Eswine writes that "desire is a firework. Handled wisely it fills the night sky with light, color, beauty, and delight. Handle desire poorly, and it can burn your neighborhood down."[1] It isn't wrong to desire good things. Things like marriage, children, meaningful work, and health aren't immoral or shameful desires, and I have prayed for all of these at various points in my life. Many of the good things in life that we long for, God gives to us. But when he doesn't immediately answer our requests, he can use waiting to train us to continue in daily faithfulness to him.

How do we maintain everyday, long-term faithfulness to Christ when we have unfulfilled desires for good things? Should we put faithfulness on hold until God answers our prayers the way we want? In a book about our faithfulness to God, we must look at the bedrock of our ability to persevere: God's faithfulness in satisfying our deepest longing. Because God has set eternity in our hearts (see Eccles. 3:11), underlying all our good desires is our deepest desire. Our hearts long to find ultimate satisfaction in God alone. David said that in God's "presence there is fullness of joy; / at [his] right hand are pleasures forevermore" (Ps. 16:11). Nothing else on earth gives us that kind of

---

1. Zack Eswine, *The Imperfect Pastor: Discovering Joy in Our Limitations through a Daily Apprenticeship with Jesus* (Wheaton, IL: Crossway, 2015), 19.

lasting joy. Until we learn contentment in God alone, we'll run far with our earthly desires and worship either their presence or their absence.

God Plus What You're Waiting For

I spent much of my adult life longing to have children. Infertility is an unwelcome companion I have never been able to distance myself from. Though my desire for children was a good one, the way I waited revealed an unbelief that God was sufficient for me. I believed God would be enough *if* he answered my prayer. I could be satisfied with God *plus* children. If God would do *this one thing*, then I could continue the path of faithful Christ-following. I'd happily study my Bible, pray with gratitude, and serve my church regularly if God would answer my request. Essentially, I planned to be "faithful" to God *plus* my fulfilled desires. But the truth is, that's idolatry. God plus anything else is idolatry.

God *plus* something else is how the Israelites in the Old Testament wandered from faithfulness to him. Think of the story of the golden calf in Exodus 32 or the ways the people repeatedly worshiped God *and* Baal throughout their history (see 1 Kings 18). They fused their worship of God with the worship of pagan deities, believing they'd find satisfaction if they fastened themselves to God *plus* a good harvest, God *plus* peace with other nations, God *plus* economic success, God *plus* fertility. Their desires for adequate food, peaceful relationships, and growing families weren't inherently wrong. But the way they waited for the fulfillment of those desires was wrong. Waiting meant demanding. And when demanding didn't work, waiting meant nudging God from his rightful place and bowing down to both their desires and their avenues of achieving them. They thought hedging their bets with idol worship would bring about fulfilled desires *just in case* God didn't answer their requests.

Waiting can quickly morph into idolatry if we aren't reminding ourselves that God is enough for us even if what we're waiting for never materializes. Everyday faithfulness trusts that the Lord can satisfy your heart when your life says otherwise.

Primed for Impatience

Our culture demands instant gains in every arena of life: knowledge, the accumulation of wealth, weight loss, intimacy. Eugene Peterson writes, "One aspect . . . I have been able to identify as harmful to Christians is the assumption that anything worthwhile can be acquired at once. We assume that if something can be done at all, it can be done quickly and efficiently. Our attention spans have been conditioned by thirty-second commercials. Our sense of reality has been flattened by thirty-page abridgments."[2]

In a culture of smartphone addiction, microwavable paleo dinner options, and Amazon Prime, we are not well-suited to wait for anything. I'd like to blame my impatience on one-day shipping and microwaves and my phone, but I know that the breeding ground for my sin is my own heart. Since Eden, we've sought to usurp God's rightful position of authority over our lives. When Satan asked Eve, "Did God actually say . . ." the temptation was to doubt that God and his commands were sufficient for the good of Adam and Eve. Since then, we've ousted his *enoughness* for any other possible answer to our longings. We settle for far less when we hang our contentment on anything other than God. In a culture that tells us we should have anything we want immediately, we find ourselves primed for impatience.

---

2. Eugene Peterson, *A Long Obedience in the Same Direction: Discipleship in an Instant Society* (Downers Grove: InterVarsity Press, 2000), 15–16.

As a result, waiting for anything feels like the wrong answer. If waiting is what we get when we ask God to fulfill a particular longing, then we assume either our desires are wrong or God must be. If we're gut-level honest, we probably question God more than ourselves. Coupling our deceitful hearts with a society of instantaneous everything, we assume waiting means something is off. But the Bible doesn't support this conclusion. Indeed, Scripture give us an entirely different view of waiting. Waiting isn't something to be avoided, and it doesn't have to derail faithfulness. Waiting is an opportunity to exercise steadfastness while you trust that God is wisely and sovereignly in control.

John Piper says, "'Waiting for the Lord' is an Old Testament way of describing the opposite of impatience. Waiting for the Lord is the opposite of running ahead of the Lord and it's the opposite of bailing out on the Lord. It's staying at your appointed place, while he says *Stay*, or it's going at his appointed pace, while he says *Go*. It's not impetuous, and it's not despairing."[3] I can think of the times I've not waited well, when my demands of the Lord included a lot of negotiating, rash decisions, and scrambling to construct a future that would resemble what I wanted. But no blessing, no trust, no growth, and no maturity is born of that kind of reckless behavior. All I accomplish in my haste to answer my own prayers is the sin of unbelief. And really, this is the crux of any discussion about waiting because what we're really talking about is satisfying an unfulfilled desire.

We like to think we shouldn't have unfulfilled longings, and if one goes unanswered, God must be asleep on the job. Or worse—he's against us. Yet Scripture sings a different song

---

3. John Piper, "Battling the Unbelief of Impatience," Desiring God website, November 27, 1988, https://www.desiringgod.org/messages/battling-the-unbelief-of-impatience/.

about waiting. The words of the Lord imply that there is good work being done in our waiting. When we find ourselves waiting for what we cannot (or should not) grasp with our own hands, we should pause to consider what God might be teaching us. He is not arbitrary in the way he answers our prayers. His continual "no" may be his way of developing the fruit of patience in your life. His perceived silence on an issue you've labored in prayer over might be the way he teaches you persistence in prayer. God doesn't withhold any good thing from us (Ps. 84:11). If your hopes for something good are long deferred, waiting may be the gift God gives you to teach you to treasure him the most. Nothing can satisfy like he does.

How Not to Wait

Consider Abraham and Sarah. God promised Abraham that he would become the father of many nations and through him all the people of the world would be blessed (see Genesis 12). For a childless old man who was closer to death than to fatherhood, waiting on God to fulfill such a promise must have felt risky. Abraham's wife, Sarah, was impatient for God's promise to materialize, and Abraham agreed to an unsavory plan Sarah stitched together to curtail any more years of waiting for what God had promised them. Offering her handmaid as proxy, Sarah sought to conceive the child God promised by other means. Ten years of waiting had passed when Sarah sent her maid to her husband's bed, but according to Genesis 16, it did not go well for anyone. The maid, Hagar, became pregnant; Sarah became jealous and sent Hagar away; and the Lord made it clear that the child of this union was not the one he had promised Abraham. Sarah ran ahead of the Lord and formulated a plan she thought would help things along. Instead of bringing about the desired child

God had promised, Sarah's plan produced a lot of grief in her household. Fifteen years later, the Lord did give Abraham and Sarah the child he had promised them. His timeline was vastly different from theirs, but his purposes were right and good.

Not every occasion of waiting-gone-wrong ends with such grievous consequences as Sarah and Abraham's attempt to hurry the Lord's hand. I can think of times when I've worked feverishly to bring about something I've waited for, and in the end things turned out *okay*, by human standards. Yet I did not trust the Lord's sovereign care for me because I was too busy pulling together a hasty way to end my waiting. My impatience did not produce spiritual growth. When pursuing an end to our unfulfilled longings become a single-minded focus, we are not only seeking to skip past what God might teach us in waiting—we also slip into idolatry. If you can think of nothing else, plan for nothing else, and pray for nothing else except the one thing you're waiting for, examine your heart. Are you trying to force the Lord's hand by taking over?

When we spend our time and devotion trying to achieve what the Lord has not brought about, we miss the blessing of spiritual maturity that comes from waiting for him. When we seek to abbreviate God-ordained waiting, we lose an opportunity to learn that he is the source of contentment. When we fixate on removing our waiting period rather than feeding on his word, we cultivate impatience rather than patience. When we stop praying for God's good purposes in favor of prayers solely dedicated to what we desire, we lose the training ground for continued growth in Christ. Waiting can be the garden where perseverance puts down strong, deep roots.

Where Perseverance Finishes the Job

Have you ever heard someone say that she's too afraid to pray for patience? Usually the statement is made as a joke about the trials that inevitably come on the heels of a prayer for God to dismantle one's impatience. We know that impatience isn't magically revoked but rather sanded down by distasteful situations that require us to wait in humility. Killing sin is always a painful process, and when it comes to suffocating the life out of our impatience, it's not a leap to expect it to hurt. We can find a biblical explanation for the work that happens in our waiting when we look at the first chapter of James.

"Count it all joy, my brothers, when you meet trials of various kinds, for you know that the testing of your faith produces steadfastness. And let steadfastness have its full effect, that you may be perfect and complete, lacking in nothing" (James 1:2–4). We'll talk about James's words on suffering in chapter 6, but don't miss what he is saying about what happens to us while we endure trials. In the midst of trials—whether of suffering or of waiting—steadfastness is being stretched and grown and made mature. Our perseverance doesn't grow in the carefree seasons of life. Perseverance is learned, owned, and grown in spite of, because of, and in the midst of difficult circumstances. Perseverance means continuing in the face of opposition. When trials come or seasons of waiting stretch out before you indefinitely, this is when perseverance gets to take effect so that you may grow in spiritual maturity.

What this kind of steadfastness looks like when you're waiting on the Lord may not be what you expect. It isn't sitting on your hands and refusing to act until the Lord changes your circumstances. Neither is it running ahead of the Lord and formulating a desired outcome. Letting steadfastness have its full effect looks more like sinking all your hope in the good character of God, knowing that he is the fixed point in all of your longings. It's pinning your contentment to his faithfulness so that if the things you pray for aren't part of his plan, then you press on with your heart still fully satisfied by God, not a potential changed circumstance. If your contentment is attached to the thing you're waiting for, then a changed circumstance is the hero of your story, not the God in whom your soul should find its deepest delight.

Waiting on relationships, reconciliation, financial peace, healing, or children might end in satisfaction of those desires. But it might not. And if your faithfulness to Christ depends on those things, then your faithfulness will only ever hinge upon a Santa Claus relationship with God. Scripture encourages us, however, to wait on the Lord to act in the ways that *he* sovereignly chooses. There is no shame in waiting on him, nor disappointment. For while we wait on him to do what is best, we learn to trust that he *does* truly know best. Robert Murray M'Cheyne writes, "God will either give you what you ask or something far better."[4] The prophet Isaiah said that "they who wait for the LORD shall renew their strength; / they shall mount up with wings like eagles; / they shall run and not be weary; / they shall walk and not faint" (Isa. 40:31). Waiting on the Lord doesn't have to wear down our faithfulness; when we trust him with our future, our perseverance strengthens.

In Psalm 62, David reminds us why it is good to wait for the Lord: "For God alone my soul waits in silence; / from him comes my salvation. / He alone is my rock and my salvation, / my fortress; I shall not be greatly shaken. . . . / Trust in him at all times, O people; / pour out your heart before him; / God is a refuge for us" (Ps. 62:1–2, 8). The one we have trusted for our salvation can certainly be trusted for our sanctification. The

---

4. Andrew Bonar, *Memoirs and Remains of the Rev. Robert Murray M'Cheyne* (Carlisle, PA: The Banner of Truth Trust, 1996), 232.

one we have trusted for our eternity in heaven can certainly be trusted with our life here on earth. He is not standing with a frowning face, doling out tiny bits of blessing to those he deems worthy. No, he delights in giving good gifts to his children! And in him we have been given every spiritual blessing in Christ (Eph. 1:3). We have forgiveness of sins and adoption as sons and daughters. We used to be his enemies. Now we're his children with an inheritance that will quiet every aching heart: God himself.

While we wait and pray, we can trust that his yeses and no's are sovereignly and lovingly part of his purposes to work good for those of us who love him.

Practically Speaking

Perhaps the most difficult part of maintaining faithfulness to Christ while you wait is knowing what to *do*. If faithful waiting isn't passive and it isn't running ahead with a plan like Sarah's, then what does it look like to wait for the Lord? How do we remain faithful when our waiting might be open-ended with no guaranteed resolution this side of heaven?

First, watch and pray. This might seem like a passive "sit on your hands" kind of approach, but prayer is not passive. Prayer acknowledges that the Lord is sovereignly in control of all things. Prayer helps us relinquish our timeline and align our desires with God's. Prayer teaches us to open our hands and submit ourselves to God's purposes.

So pray often as you wait, and do pray about your deferred hopes. But don't pray only that God will give you what you're waiting for. Pray that your heart will be most satisfied in him. Pray that you'll treasure him more than your answered prayers. Pray that you'll learn contentment in him while you wait. Pray that he might use you for his kingdom whether or not he gives you what you ask for. Pray that you'll trust him with your life. Pray for his will to be done, as Jesus instructed (see Matt. 6:10). Look at what God is doing in your life that's good, and praise him for it. Watch for opportunities to minister to others who are waiting.

As you pray according to God's desires, make decisions for your life with the belief that God is in control, not you. Seek wise counsel from more seasoned believers like your pastors or a mentor. Take next steps but hold your plans loosely, knowing God may change them. This might mean being open to an option you did not previously want to consider because it didn't factor into your life's plan. Build accountability into your life so you don't make decisions out of fear or that reflect you're in a hurry to get to the next thing.

Waiting for children during my years of infertility felt embarrassing at times. I couldn't control my future, and I felt the sting of being *less than* others who had what I desired. Here's what I wish someone would have said to me: do not feel ashamed while you wait for the Lord. With Christ you have all you need. You're not *less than* because you don't have something you long for. Undesired singleness, childlessness, "dead end" jobs, strained finances—none of these mean you are lacking what matters most. Psalm 25:3 says, "Indeed, none who wait for you shall be put to shame; / they shall be ashamed who are wantonly treacherous." Shame comes from sin, not from waiting on the Lord. If he stays his hand in fulfilling a deferred hope, you must not equate your worth or your joy in what you feel you lack. Both your worth and joy are ever secure in Christ. No deferred hope can rob you of this truth!

Finally, make yourself happy in the Lord. Perhaps this seems like an abstract idea, but the concrete ways of making yourself happy in God are accomplished in the expressions of faithfulness we've discussed throughout this book so far. Read God's word, pray to the Lord, and remain committed to the body of Christ through local church involvement. You can shift your gaze away from what you lack and toward Christ, who fulfills the deepest yearnings of your heart. Fixate on God's faithful character by saturating your heart with Scripture and keep a record of the spiritual blessings he has given you in Christ. Write down the ways he has lavished you with grace upon grace. Practice gratitude so you don't miss the ways he has met your needs in the past.

You can reduce your tunnel vision (which we're all apt to have when we're waiting for something) by seeking to serve others. Look around at those in your church and community who have needs you can meet. You'll not only turn your eyes away from yourself, but perhaps you will be the vessel God uses to end another person's season of waiting.

Waiting is a gift none of us want. We avoid it because it's painful and slow. And it may be a cause for grief when you never see the things you pray for come to fruition. I think of Hannah in 1 Samuel whose infertility had etched her face in grief. On a yearly visit to the temple, she prayed with tears and anguish—so much so that the priest thought she was either drunk or out of her mind. After laying bare her heart before God, she went her way, ate, and her face was no longer sad (see 1 Sam. 1:1–18). Hannah embraced grief for the life she had waited for but had not received. After pouring out her heart to the Lord, however, she refused to let her grief define her. John Piper advises us to both acknowledge our grief when we do not get the life we had hoped for and see God's goodness to us even in what we lack:

> Sixty years go by, and forty years on you think, "I've come to terms with that," and then one morning it breaks over

you, and you weep about a 40-year old loss, or a 40-year "never have," and my counsel is, yes, go ahead, embrace that moment. Weep.

But then, say to your weeping after a season, "No. You will not define me, sorrow, because my God has said, 'No good thing does he withhold from those who walk upright' (Ps. 84:11). Therefore, even though it was good in one sense, and I miss it in one sense, I trust my God, and he has not withheld anything that is good for me." Yes, let there be weeping in those seasons—feel the losses. Then wash your face, trust God, and embrace the life he's given you.[5]

The Lord loves you, friend, and while waiting doesn't always feel pleasant, he does not work harm in your waiting. God can cultivate deep trust in him as you wait. He is teaching you to persevere and to treasure him the most. He has ordained all of your days, and you can trust him with every single one.

---

5. John Piper. "Embrace the Life God Has Given You," Desiring God website, March 10, 2017, https://www.desiringgod.org/embrace-the-life-god-has-given-you/.

Faithful Like Sue

Sue spent most of her adult life as a stay-at-home mom and ministry wife. Her husband had long served as a worship leader in the local church, and together they raised two girls to follow Christ and love the church. As Sue and her husband approached their retirement years, her husband abruptly lost his job, and they spent the next several years looking for a job that would provide for them. In the midst of their years of instability, they lost everything in an apartment fire. Often, Sue longed for the Lord to bring them to a phase of life when they did not have to wonder what was coming next.

In her sixties, Sue went back to work for the first time in thirty years. She spent what would have been her retirement years working in the public school system, as did her husband. Sue could have chosen bitterness rather than gratitude. She could have complained about how tired she was at the end of each workday during what should have been years of rest, but she didn't.

Sue worked without complaint and viewed her classroom as a mission field until a serious illness forced her to give up her job. Even with regular treatments and doctor's appointments, Sue spent her spare time serving others and sacrificing time and money to invest in both her local church and several missionary families. Quietly, without fanfare and without accolades, Sue held fast to Christ as her anchor and found strength to persevere through prayer, God's word, and her church. Though Sue has waited long for her circumstances to change, many have been encouraged by her quiet faithfulness and generosity of love and care as she has waited. Indeed, she points others to Christ with her quiet way of selfless service.

5

Faithful When You Doubt

"How can I have assurance of my faith in Christ?" My friend's voice wobbled on the other end of the phone call. Her voice thick with tears, she explained that listening to a sermon at church had brought deep conviction about her approach to sin. "I can't seem to find a middle ground. I'm either too callous toward my sin or so concerned about it, I can't function for fear that I'm not truly saved."

Though I've had the privilege of watching this friend blossom in maturing faith in Jesus for a decade, I didn't brush off her question. Her desperation for assurance brought back many memories of lying in my bed at night throughout my teenage years when I prayed the sinner's prayer over and over again just in case I didn't mean it enough the last time or had sinned too much that day. "Now I lay me down to sleep, I pray the Lord my soul to keep, and Lord, will you please save me in case I'm not really saved?"

Over the course of my young years, I must have asked Jesus into my heart a hundred times in fear that I would somehow miss true conversion or that God would rescind his offer of salvation to me. I understood my friend's paralyzing fear of judgment and eternity in hell. I'd felt it pressing on my chest on nights I couldn't sleep. And what if I died in my sleep? Better pray again just in case.

Hope for the Scrupulous Conscience

The believer's fear of judgment often plagues what Christian psychologist Ed Welch calls "the scrupulous conscience."[1] (Knowing that there is an actual term for this helps us to rest easy, knowing we're not alone in our struggle. As 1 Corinthians 10:13 assures us: "No temptation has overtaken you that is not common to man.") A believer with a scrupulous conscience does what my friend had been doing, which was to fear that patterns of sin in her life proved a lack of faith in Christ. The answer isn't to ignore sin altogether; after all, the Holy Spirit works to *keep* the believer from ignoring sin. So what do we do when our faithfulness is threatened by doubts that we are really "in Christ"?

Throughout this chapter, we'll discuss God's role in our salvation, how we can know our soul is secure in him, and how everyday faithfulness aids us in assurance. Whether you doubt your salvation sometimes or all the time, you'll walk away with both encouragement of God's promise to finish what he started as well as the tools to help you believe him.

We Can Trust God

Some of our fear of not being "really saved" is rooted in a misunderstanding of our role in conversion and, after that, in our sanctification. We must repent and believe to be saved, but even these acts of obedience are kind gifts of grace from God.

---

1. Edward T. Welch, *Running Scared: Fear, Worry, and the God of Rest* (Greensboro, NC: New Growth Press, 2007), 219.

Paul said, "For by grace you have been saved through faith. And this is not your own doing; it is the gift of God, not a result of works, so that no one may boast" (Eph. 2:8–9). When you "confess with your mouth that Jesus is Lord and believe in your heart that God raised him from the dead, you will be saved" (Rom. 10:9). Bottom line: you must believe in Christ and repent from your sins to be saved, but it is *God* who first makes you alive in Christ so that you can do so.

God is the one who makes your dead heart beat for him. He gives you both the faith to believe and the obedience to repent (see Rom. 2:4; Acts 11:18). He makes you a new creation. He transfers you from the domain of darkness to the kingdom of Jesus (see Col. 1:13). God first does the work of regeneration—of making us alive in Christ—so that we may have faith to believe that Jesus is Lord and that God raised him from the dead. We respond in obedience to the transforming work of the gospel with repentance and belief, but we do not do it apart from God's power and plan.

Do you see that your salvation doesn't depend on you? If you have repented and believed, it is because God has made your heart alive in order to do so! Paul gives us great encouragement about the transformative work happening in our salvation. It began long before you believed. "And those whom he predestined he also called, and those whom he called he also justified, and those whom he justified he also glorified" (Rom. 8:30). God planned to save you. Paul tells us in Ephesians 1:4 that God's plan for those he would save was in place before the world began. God planned to save you, he called you to faith through the gospel, and he justified you, making you righteous before him (see 2 Cor. 5:21). And God's promise of your glorification (freedom from sinning forever in heaven) is so sure and certain that Paul uses the past tense to describe it.

Here's what I want you to take away from this discussion of salvation and repentance and belief: those whom God has purposed to save will be saved, and they will persevere in their faith because God is invested in their perseverance. If he has saved you, he will not leave his work in your life unfinished. He will certainly finish what he has started. As we've seen in Philippians, he has promised to bring his work to completion (Phil.1:6). We can trust him!

It Is Finished

Perhaps you know you can trust God, but what if you can't trust *you*? Maybe your belief wasn't sincere or maybe you sin too much. When I was a teenager, I struggled to recall the exact moment of my conversion, which had taken place when I was a child. I fretted constantly about whether my faith was sincere enough in the past. I didn't understand that the faith with which I believed the gospel was a gift from God, and I did not have to doubt if God-given faith was sincere enough.

If a worry about sincere faith isn't your issue, perhaps you fear your sin will keep you from persevering in faith. Is it possible to undo God's work of salvation?

An encouraging tone of finality permeates the New Testament language of salvation. The most obvious example is Jesus's final words at the cross: "It is finished" (John 19:30). In those three words, Jesus proclaimed that the work the Father sent him to do was complete. He paid the penalty for our sins and then gave up his spirit. His death accomplished our redemption and gave us freedom from sin.

Paul paints a vivid picture of what happened at the cross:

> And you, who were dead in your trespasses and the uncircumcision of your flesh, God made alive together with him, having forgiven us all our trespasses, by canceling

the record of debt that stood against us with its legal demands. This he set aside, nailing it to the cross. He disarmed the rulers and authorities and put them to open shame, by triumphing over them in him. (Col. 2:13–15)

Here's the finality I'm talking about: picture the record of your sins against God printed out on a piece of paper. Think of it as your lifetime criminal record that has earned you the death penalty, with all its ugly and damning indictments. It's a long list, I know. But now picture Jesus taking your lengthy criminal record and nailing it to the cross. See a big red stamp across the front that says "Debt canceled. Paid in full by a mediator."

If the debt has been paid by someone else, then the debt collector has no reason to hold your debt against you. You are the debtor. Jesus is the payor. And God is the debt collector who loves both you and Jesus and is pleased to accept Jesus's payment for your sin. He will not reject his Son's sacrifice! To prove it, God did three extraordinary things that should give us assurance and confidence to press forward in faith.

First, after the great exchange that took place at the cross, God imputed Christ's righteousness to us. *Imputation* means that God not only transferred (or counted) our sin and guilt to Christ, but also that God credits us with Christ's righteousness. Because Jesus paid for our sin at the cross, we get to wear his righteousness. Hold this truth close to your heart when the shame of past sins chokes your faith: when God looks at you, he now sees Jesus. You have nothing to fear because there is no more judgment for you—there is no more condemnation (see Rom. 8:1). Every drop of wrath your sin has earned was borne by your Savior, and he gave you his holiness and purity to wear. Elyse Fitzpatrick writes, "There's no more wrath to be had. His disposition toward you today is what it has been since he made you his own: he loves you and longs for you to know it and savor every drop of it."[2] You can follow Christ in faithfulness because you get to claim his perfect record!

Second, God raised Jesus from the dead. The resurrection is proof that Jesus's payment for our sins was enough for our right standing before God. Paul said that Jesus was "delivered up for our trespasses and raised for our justification" (Rom. 4:25). Jesus's resurrection is also a promise that *you* will be resurrected one day. "For as in Adam all die, so also in Christ shall all be made alive. But each in his own order: Christ the firstfruits, then at his coming those who belong to Christ" (1 Cor. 15:22–23). Again—finality. Jesus's death and resurrection secure your eternity.

The third thing God did to prove that the debt against you has been canceled at the cross was to send the Holy Spirit as a guarantee that we have an eternal inheritance with God in heaven. "In [Christ] you also, when you heard the word of truth, the gospel of your salvation, and believed in him, were sealed with the promised Holy Spirit, who is the guarantee of our inheritance until we acquire possession of it, to the praise of his glory" (Eph. 1:13–14). The Spirit is given to every believer until we are with God face-to-face. He convicts us of sin, enables us to obey his word, and intercedes for us to God. Because he lives in us, we can be certain that we'll gain our eternal inheritance in heaven, which is God himself.

Your salvation, sanctification, and future glorification have been secured by all three members of the Trinity. God has gone to great lengths to safeguard your present perseverance and your future inheritance. You can trust that your salvation has been secured by him. Your response to this gift is obedience—not to *earn* that security but *because* of the security.

---

2. Elyse Fitzpatrick, *Because He Loves Me: How Christ Transforms Our Daily Life* (Wheaton, IL: Crossway, 2008), 91.

Everyday Repentance

For some of us, the ongoing struggle with sin drives our fear of judgment. We worry that we should be much farther along in godliness, that we shouldn't be sinning so much. This was the fear my friend was battling when she called me in a panic. Perhaps you ask similar questions. Shouldn't I be sinning less by now? If I have truly repented of my sins, wouldn't I have moved away from them? These questions can cripple us with fear when we're trying to follow Jesus but can't seem to escape our constant doubts. I've asked them myself, on several occasions. Most of the time, I find that I'm functioning on a faulty understanding of repentance.

Once when I was in Sunday school as a child, a teacher stood in front of the class and demonstrated what repentance looks like. She defined it as turning away from your sin, and illustrated it by walking in one direction then suddenly turning around and walking in the opposite direction. It's a helpful picture, and one I've used many times with my own children. Yet on some level I thought that once someone believed the gospel and made that one-hundred-eighty-degree turn, that person was done with repentance. Or she should be. John's words in his first epistle made me worry: "No one who abides in [God] keeps on sinning; no one who keeps on sinning has either seen him or known him" (1 John 3:6). What? Was I deceiving myself about my true state before God? Would a continual struggle with sin disqualify me from heaven? Why didn't my first act of repentance take permanent effect when I became a Christian?

John's words do warn us that believers will not make a habit of sin, but his words should also comfort us. Just a chapter earlier, John said that he wrote his epistle so that the recipients wouldn't sin, but *if they did*, they would know they had Christ as an advocate (see 1 John 2:1–2). John Stott writes, "Thus, the Father's provision for the sinning Christian is in his Son. . . . [A Christian] may sin sometimes, even with the consent of the mind and the will, but he is overwhelmed by grief and repentance afterwards (Ps. 51)."[3] And because we have Christ as an advocate, we respond with regular repentance. Faithfulness isn't just one, single, about-face turn. The faithful Christian life is made up of everyday turning, everyday repentance. In a sermon on John 3, Jeff Medders explains that the Christian repents of sin daily to realign himself with Christ daily.[4] The one-hundred-eighty-degree turn at conversion was meant to become a lifestyle of turns. So rather than fearing that you should be perfect by now (you won't be until heaven), ask yourself about what you're running after the most. As Welch asks, "Which direction do you face? Is your face turned toward Christ or away from him?"[5] A person facing Christ will repent, turn to God, and bear fruit in keeping with repentance (see Matt. 3:8; Acts 26:20). Ongoing repentance keeps a Christian facing Jesus rather than her sin, and she'll bear fruit that demonstrates which direction she's facing.

No Wasted Pruning

It's hard to struggle with assurance, particularly if doubt becomes a regular state of mind. Perhaps you wonder why you're plagued with this particular issue so much. I encourage you to look at this with a different lens. Awareness of your sin can help you fight it, which is a crucial part of remaining faithful to Christ, as we'll see in chapter 8. A continual examination

3. John R.W. Stott, *The Letters of John* (Downers Grove, IL: InterVarsity Press, 1988), 89, 139.

4. Jeff Medders, "Hear the Voices: Why the Baptist and a Baptism Matter to You," Redeemer Church website, January 6, 2019, http://www.makingmuchofjesus.org/sermons/sermon/2019-01-06/hear-the-voices:-why-the-baptist-and-a-baptism-matter-to-you/.

5. Welch, *Running Scared*, 218.

of your heart's motives can be a form of pruning. And those practices may help you see that you are, in fact, in Christ.

But when your concerns for your status before God paralyze you with fear, Ed Welch says to "be suspicious about your fears. Doesn't it make sense that, if you are that concerned about your citizenship in the kingdom, this interest has been sparked by the Spirit himself? Any interest anyone has in Jesus Christ is not natural to us. It is stirred by God himself."[6] God may bring your attention to a particular area of sin so that you can confess and practice repentance. Pruning is not something to be avoided or bemoaned but rather something that should warm you with confidence that God is currently keeping his promises to make you more like Jesus.

God doesn't prune what is destined for the fire. In all the agrarian examples of sifting between believers and unbelievers in the New Testament, it's the chaff, the stubble, the weeds that are destined for the fires of judgment, not the wheat or vines that have been carefully tended by the farmer or vineyard keeper (see Matt. 13:30, 40–42; John 15:6). When Jesus speaks of being attached to the vine in John 15, he gives us a clear picture of the purpose of pruning. It's to bear more fruit! "Every branch in me that does not bear fruit [the Father] takes away, and every branch that does bear fruit he prunes, that it may bear more fruit" (John 15:2).

Pruning is the process of cutting away dead parts of a vine or tree so that fruitfulness and growth are increased. It might seem counterproductive to cut a vine or remove a branch to *increase* growth, but the removal of the dead or diseased parts is what allows the plant to thrive. So when God reveals the parts of your life that need to be removed for growth, see it as the outworking of his promise to sanctify you, not a reason to

---

6. Welch, *Running Scared*, 220.

question if you're in Christ. His pruning is purposeful and for our good. It won't be wasted on a heart that is unconcerned with sin or judgment. Jesus said that anyone who does not abide in him "is thrown away like a branch and withers; and the branches are gathered, thrown into the fire, and burned" (John 15:6). But those that are pruned to bear fruit will glorify God. Pruning will encourage your perseverance and bring about spiritual maturity.

Practically Speaking

Jesus's pruning metaphor in John 15 gives us some practical ways to address our struggle for assurance. The expressions of faithfulness that propel us through busy seasons and periods of waiting are the same ones that will help us fight our fears of judgment when we are already in Christ:

> Abide in me, and I in you. As the branch cannot bear fruit by itself, unless it abides in the vine, neither can you, unless you abide in me. I am the vine; you are the branches. Whoever abides in me and I in him, he it is that bears much fruit, for apart from me you can do nothing. If anyone does not abide in me he is thrown away like a branch and withers; and the branches are gathered, thrown into the fire, and burned. If you abide in me, and my words abide in you, ask whatever you wish, and it will be done for you. By this my Father is glorified, that you bear much fruit and so prove to be my disciples. As the Father has loved me, so have I loved you. Abide in my love. (John 15:4–9)

We see Jesus's instructions to abide in him (which leads to fruit-bearing) exercised in the individual spiritual disciplines and the corporate ones. Though it isn't always easy, abiding in him is not a complicated thing. To use Jesus's vine/branch imagery, abiding means being attached to him. And being attached to him means feeding your faithfulness to him with what he has given us. Friends, we always come back to his good words that fill up the pages of our Bibles. Remember, Jesus tells us that the way we love him and remain in his love is to obey his commandments (John 14:15). Obedience to his commandments cannot be done apart from knowing what those commandments are and building our life around them.

The way you abide in Christ today is the way you had to abide in Christ yesterday, and the way you will abide in him tomorrow. You remain attached to him by seeking him in Scripture, in prayer, and in bearing fruit. God will cultivate fruit when you are firmly attached to his Son. Regular repentance, turning your face to Jesus, fighting sin, feeding yourself with the nourishment of his word—these are the ways you abide in Christ, knowing that as you abide in him, God is keeping his promise to complete the work he began when he saved you. The fruit that grows as a result of your continual abiding will be evidence of faithfulness that glorifies God. You might struggle to see the fruit, but others won't.

When you are plagued by doubts, your perseverance can be greatly aided by the local church. Most of us will find it difficult to gauge our own spiritual growth, especially if we have a scrupulous conscience. But regular connection to your church can provide you with faithful shepherding and oversight, biblical teaching, and relationships that both contribute to your growth and help you see it rightly. Additionally, you'll be encouraged when you see the Lord sustain other believers in the body through their struggles and fears.

If you worry that you're not growing or bearing fruit, ask someone from church who knows you well to explore with you areas where she sees spiritual maturity. I couldn't chart an unbiased graph of my own growth in Christ (because I definitely have a scrupulous conscience), but when I picture the faces of my fellow church members, I can easily see the ways they've blossomed in their relationship with Christ, how they love him more now than they did five years ago, how they've matured in their faith. The fruit they are bearing is unmistakably obvious. I see their fruit, and as their fellow church member I benefit from it. Their faithfulness encourages mine.

That day my friend called me in fear for her soul, I asked her who else she was talking to about her concerns. We don't live in the same city, and I wanted to be sure her church community knew what was going on. A week later, as we continued to work through the Bible, she shared that she was having regular conversations about her doubts with her husband, her pastor's wife, and her small group from church.

As the days passed, I listened to her work through her fears and examine them in light of Scripture. With the encouragement of the leadership and members of her church and a lot of prayer and searching God's word, she was able to see what was true about her salvation and her status before the Father.

Our doubts often lose their power when we speak them out loud to our brothers and sisters in Christ. If you're struggling alone with doubts about your salvation, please ask the Lord for the courage to speak to another believer about it. Ask your pastor, your women's ministry leader, a mentor, a Sunday school teacher, your small group leader, or the woman who sits behind you in church. Let the body of Christ help you examine your fears without blowing them out of proportion. Let them pray for you, speak truth to you, encourage you, and point you to God's word.

As you examine your heart, don't get caught up in past faith. Sometimes that question of past sincerity can rob us of all confidence that we are truly in Christ. Rather, ask yourself this: Do I believe in the saving work of Jesus *today*? Am I following him *now*? Am I facing Christ this moment? If not, repent again and turn your face toward Jesus. He will sustain you when you wake up tomorrow to turn your face toward him again.

Faithful Like Beth

Beth grew up in the church and came to faith in Christ as a child. She attended a Christian university, married a man bound for church ministry, and taught elementary school before starting a family. Having grown in her faith under solid teaching at church and in her personal Bible study, Beth was passionate for the women in her church to love the word of God. Though she was younger than most of the women in her church, she taught studies and encouraged others to be involved in both personal and corporate spiritual disciplines.

Beth's growth in Christ was obvious to those who knew her well. She had moved from milk to meat, which fed her zeal for others to have the same experience of growth. Regularly plugged into church, mentoring relationships, and ministry, Beth was surprised when she began questioning her salvation. Suddenly, all her involvements didn't seem to matter if she couldn't attain a "more righteous" status before God. She was certain she should be farther along in faith than she was at the time.

Rather than draw into her doubts and lose hope in internal processing, Beth reached out to the believers in her life who knew her well and who knew God's word well. Though she had trouble sleeping at night and though she was afraid that reading her Bible each day would feed her fear of judgment, she continued searching the scriptures to help her understand what was true about the security of her soul. Beth voiced her concerns and explored them within the community of faith, letting her church know about her struggles. Even though she felt exposed, Beth didn't keep her fears to herself. The body of Christ comforted, encouraged, directed, and prayed for her.

At the end of her season of doubt, Beth concluded that the process of working through Scripture and sharing her burden with others had been good for her soul. She'd seen areas of sin that needed to be addressed, and she'd allowed others to point out the fruit the Lord had grown in her life that she had failed to see herself. But mostly, Beth learned that perseverance is possible when God has made you alive in Christ and given you the faith to believe the gospel.

6

Faithful When You're Suffering

When I was young, I thought following Jesus meant I'd never have to suffer. I'm not sure where I picked up that sort of thinking. In my youthful experience, suffering was for either the really bad people or the really, really holy ones. I aimed to land somewhere just far enough past "really bad" to avoid suffering for sinful choices but just shy of "really, really holy" so I wouldn't ever show up in a modern version of *Foxe's Book of Martyrs*. Average Christ-following (nothing fanatic) should ensure me a trouble-free existence, right?

My desire for average Christ-following was evidence that I hadn't yet read my Bible enough to know that suffering and Christ-following go hand in hand. We suffer not because we're really bad or really, really holy but because as believers we're living in enemy-occupied territory on a planet that groans for Christ's return. Jesus himself said, "In the world you will have tribulation" (John 16:33).

The theology of suffering deserves its own discussion, and indeed there are many well-written books to choose from on the subject, but for the purposes of this chapter, I'll simplify things.[1] Sometimes we suffer because we sin, sometimes we suffer because others sin, and sometimes we suffer without ever knowing a reason for it. Suffering that we did not bring upon ourselves is most difficult to reconcile, and yet it provides a framework that the writers of the Bible deemed necessary for becoming like Christ and learning perseverance.

Even as an adult, the guarantee of suffering for the Christian rubs me the wrong way. Yet when I look at my own experiences with infertility and chronic pain, I know how God can use our deepest sorrows to teach us to hold fast to him. What's more, he uses them to teach us that he is holding fast to us. I might have been more prepared to persevere through trials had I understood that there are some things we learn as believers that can only be revealed in the fires of suffering. Jesus promised it, James assumed it, Peter guaranteed it, and Paul spoke of it often. Remaining faithful to Christ in the midst of suffering requires that we cease being surprised by the arrival of our trials.

When You Suffer

"*When*, not if," I said to my Bible study group. They nodded solemnly; they'd seen it, too. We were studying the book of James, and as we gathered around a small table at the local coffee shop to discuss the first chapter, we discovered we all had a little trouble moving past the opening verses written by Jesus's half brother. "Count it all joy, my brothers, when you meet trials of various kinds" (James 1:2). *When*. Not if.

---

1. I recommend the following books on suffering: D. A. Carson, *How Long, O Lord: Reflections on Suffering and Evil*, 2nd ed. (Grand Rapids, MI: Baker Academic, 2006); Elisabeth Elliot, *Your Suffering Is Never for Nothing* (Nashville, TN: B&H, 2019); Dave Furman, *Kiss the Wave: Embracing God in Your Trials* (Wheaton, IL: Crossway, 2018); David Powlison, *God's Grace in Your Suffering* (Wheaton, IL: Crossway, 2018); Mark Vroegop, *Dark Clouds, Deep Mercy: Discovering the Grace of Lament* (Wheaton, IL: Crossway, 2019); Paul David Tripp, *Suffering: Gospel Hope When Life Doesn't Make Sense* (Wheaton, IL: Crossway, 2018).

Peter said it differently, though just as plainly: "Beloved, do not be surprised at the fiery trial when it comes upon you to test you, as though something strange were happening to you" (1 Pet. 4:12). When, not if. He goes further by telling believers to rejoice in the suffering that we should expect. "But rejoice insofar as you share Christ's sufferings, that you may also rejoice and be glad when his glory is revealed" (1 Pet. 4:13). Not only should we expect to suffer as believers; we should also see it as an opportunity to rejoice that we can become more like Christ through our trials. In so doing, our joy will be multiplied when he is glorified in our lives.

When our eyes are trained on the glory of Christ, we can not only endure suffering but actually rejoice in it. How does that even work? How do we rejoice when we're in pain, when disease robs us of our loved ones, when loneliness wets our pillows with tears? What joy is there to be had in circumstances that leach all the happiness out of our lives?

Paul helps us understand the *how* by explaining what's happening in our suffering: "Not only that, but we rejoice in our sufferings, knowing that suffering produces endurance, and endurance produces character, and character produces hope, and hope does not put us to shame, because God's love has been poured into our hearts through the Holy Spirit who has been given to us" (Rom. 5:3–5). Keeping our eyes on Christ and the hope we have in him helps us persevere. Paul goes on to talk about what Jesus did that makes that hope so hopeful: he died for us while we were still dead in our sins. The gospel helps us press on. Studying Christ's faithfulness aids us in ours. And the Holy Spirit, who lives in us, works to bring forth fruitfulness from our suffering.

I've heard people grapple with the question of joy in suffering by explaining that joy comes *after* the fact or when we look back at all we learned. And I do think there is truth to that. But the New Testament writers seem to be talking about joy in the *midst* of pain and grief. To be honest, that sounds impossible. And yet, if our joy—our contentment, rest, and peace—hinges upon the unchangeable person and work of Christ, then joy *is* something we can hold on to when our circumstances are splintering around us. Joy is not a circumstance; joy is a person. Life may sway with uncertainty, but Jesus never will. He does not disappoint.

Already His, Not Yet Home

When we're aching with loss or fighting daily pain, it's difficult to comprehend holding joy in one hand and suffering in the other. By earthly standards, it's sufficient to hold survival and nothing else with both hands. But suffering can produce more than just survival when the Christian keeps the end in mind. (And as we discussed in chap. 3, survival for the Christian *is* holding on to Christ.) This gritty place between pain and glory is where perseverance gets to do its best work. It pulls us through the other side with eyes that are trained on the Lord. The lenses we're looking through really matter. Suffering looks different when we can see far enough to glimpse the glory of the coming kingdom.

When propped against the eternal glory we have in heaven with God, our sufferings are a warm breath on a cold day. A puff of air that's burned off quickly. Paul explains in Romans 8:18: "For I consider that the sufferings of this present time are not worth comparing with the glory that is to be revealed to us." Our trials may feel a lot bigger than just a breath, but we must remember that this life is not all there is. Our best life as believers begins later, and it will be free from all the things that plague us with sorrows and grief. We can endure because this is not our home. God may use pain to sharpen our faith in the fact that he will carry us through. A sharpened faith results in hope that never disappoints.

We live in an "already-not yet" tension. Yes, Jesus's kingdom has come, but it is coming still. Yes, we have been redeemed by his work at the cross and reconciled to the Father, but we still suffer heartache, disease, loss, grief, and sin. We live on the same earth God created back in Genesis that now groans with yearning for a happy ending, but one day we'll live in a new heaven and a new earth where sorrows cannot follow us to our happiest of endings. The grand gospel story has two big finishes—one at the cross and the empty tomb, and one that ends with the people of God living forever in his presence. We're now living in that part of the story between the two big finishes.

While we live in the tension of *already his* but *not yet home*, we must labor to see our grief and sufferings as the means by which the Lord will prove himself faithfully near to us while we're here. They are reminders that he is with us now, but we'll be with him later. And the later, the not-yet part, is where our real citizenship is found. Look ahead and know this isn't all there is. Paul's admonishment in Colossians 3:2 reminds us to keep our gaze fixed on the coming glory, of the future that awaits us: "Set your minds on things that are above, not on things that are on earth." What is above has a deeper impact than what's on the earth.

When we finish James's words about the *when* of suffering, we find that the result of perseverance is maturity in Christ: "Count it all joy, my brothers, when you meet trials of various kinds, for you know that the testing of your faith produces steadfastness. And let steadfastness have its full effect, that you may be perfect and complete, lacking in nothing" (James 1:2–4). God can use our suffering to make us more like Christ, but it isn't necessarily an overnight kind of change. Endurance through trials is one of the tools God will use to burn off the sins of entitlement or self-sufficiency and teach us that he is our greatest need. That refining fire that Peter talks about can reveal a steadfast hope that endures sorrow and suffering.

Looking forward to the coming hope of heaven and looking back at what we've learned in our trials helps us keep our vision in check. It makes our sufferings something we can endure for the sake of becoming like Christ.

No One Wants to Be Job

God has given us an entire book of the Bible dedicated to the story of one man's incredible losses. Job is the one many of us think of when it comes to suffering or patience in grief, but none of us want to be Job. We want to learn the lessons of endurance without attending the school of suffering. And that's understandable! Job's life plays out like a real-life Greek tragedy. But in God's kindness, we have Job's story as both a glimpse of what God might be doing in our suffering and a clear view of how we can persevere through it.

In the beginning of Job's story, we learn that Job is an incredibly wealthy, God-fearing father who is keenly aware of the dangerous effects of sin. He fears God and turns away from evil, but he also offers sacrifices to God for his grown children who may have sinned in their feasting and enjoyment of prosperity (see Job 1:1–5). Early in the story, we read about a conversation between God and Satan. God is certain that nothing Satan can do to Job will minimize his faith, but Satan suggests that Job's allegiance to God is tethered to his happy circumstances. Wealth, family, health—all are good reasons to love the God who gave them to you. But, Satan suggests,

Faithful When You're Suffering   103

take those blessings away and see what Job's faith is really made of. God grants Satan permission to do anything he likes to Job except to take his life. So off Satan goes to rob Job of his children, his wealth, and his health.

All of this takes place in the first two chapters of Job, and at the end of chapter 2, we find Job covered in sores and sitting in ashes, looking so unlike himself that his friends who come to visit don't recognize him. For seven days and nights Job's friends sit in silence with him, "for they saw that his suffering was very great" (Job 2:13). Eventually, though, the friends speak up, and what they have to say isn't very helpful. They search for meaning in Job's suffering, hopeful for a place to cast blame. Inevitably, they look to Job's sin as a reason for his suffering. Yet we know from the beginning that Job's suffering wasn't a result of his sin but of his faithfulness to God, and that God allowed that faithfulness to be tested.

Back and forth they go in the conversation—Job, his friends, and eventually God himself. Job cycles through his grief with questions about God and to God but does not give up his faith in God. "I hold fast my righteousness and will not let it go," Job says (Job 27:6). When the Lord addresses Job, he points Job to his character, power, and might. God draws Job's eyes away from the ashes, the sores, the losses, and toward God's power in creating the universe, in his sovereignty over creation, and in his awareness of every tiny, insignificant thing that happens on this earth. The God who made and holds the cosmos together knows the life span of every animal roaming in the wild (see Job 39). We can almost hear Jesus's voice in God's response to Job: "Are you not of more value than they?" (Matt. 6:26).

Job's suffering didn't happen apart from God's sovereign hand, and though the reasons for our suffering may never be apparent to us (Job didn't know!), we can entrust ourselves—

every molecule of our disease-ridden bodies and every emotion of our lamenting hearts—to the one who holds the universe in his hands. If he has deemed it necessary that we should suffer, we can trust him for the good he will surely work from it. Job's faithfulness wasn't shattered in his suffering. It was strengthened. Sores and sorrows may have picked at the threads of Job's faith, but meditating on the immovable, unshakable character of God held it together.

When everything was still bleak and dark in Job's life, it was focusing on God's faithfulness that encouraged Job's perseverance. He said to the Lord, "I know that you can do all things, / and that no purpose of yours can be thwarted" (Job 42:2). We know that God's purpose for us is to make us more like Jesus.

Practically Speaking

Maybe you're holding this book in hands that ache with rheumatoid arthritis or are scarred with needle sticks from multiple hospitalizations. Maybe you've skipped ahead to this chapter because you recently buried someone you love and can't imagine what it looks like to hold fast to Jesus when your heart hurts this much. What then? Does perseverance matter, or should you just try to survive and let the spiritual chips of your growth in Christ fall where they will?

We cannot know how long our seasons of suffering might last, but if we abandon our faithfulness to Christ when trials come, we will miss the ways he is being faithful to us in our suffering. The good news is that he has given us his word, his Spirit, and his church to help us persevere through our darkest days. We'll spend a bit more time in this section to see how God equips us to press forward in faith by keeping our eyes on him.

Pain and grief can make spiritual disciplines like Bible reading or prayer quite challenging. Physical pain has a way of setting up residence in your mind and letting nothing else in. Grief crowds out every thought but the one that makes your heart ache the most. Here is where years of past faithfulness can serve you during your present suffering. If your life has been built around the habitual expressions of faith, don't give up on them now. Let your default response continually be one that leads you to God's word. You need it now more than ever.

Perhaps all you can do is sit with your Bible open and ask why. That's a good beginning. Open God's word to the places that have ministered to you in the past and remember that God has not changed even though your life has. Ask questions of him in his word. If all you can do is look for what the Scripture tells you about God's character, it will be well worth the effort. When your pain makes you fear that God has forgotten you, Scripture reminds you that he is with you (Ps. 23:4). When grief crowds your heart with sorrow, the Bible tells you that God is intimately aware of every tear (Ps. 56:8). If illness makes you fear what the future holds, you can know for sure that you are secure in God's love for you (Rom. 8:38–39).

Like Job, shift your gaze from your painful circumstances to the sovereign and good character of God so you can view those circumstances correctly. We might wrestle with the reasons for our suffering, but much of the time it is not for us to know why. My pastor friend Lee Tankersley said in a sermon once, "We do not have to know God's plans to walk in peace. It should be enough to know *him*."[2] Rest in the fact that God has given you everything you need to persevere, even if you never have an answer to the *why* of your suffering. "Oh, the depths of

---

2. Lee Tankersley, "The Promises, Plans, and Presence of God" (sermon on Joshua 1–5, September 23, 2018).

the riches and wisdom and knowledge of God! How unsearchable are his judgments and how inscrutable his ways!" Paul reminds us (Rom. 11:33). We can trust in God's wisdom even if we don't understand it.

Read through the psalms and see how the psalmists are comforted in crises by truths about God's character. In the psalms, the people of God express a range of emotions, and they plead for help in many different kinds of trials. Meditating on God's character reminded them of his steadfast love for them and helped them to persevere. When you read the psalms, look for how God loves his people. He doesn't always remove them from their afflictions, but he never abandons them. He is with his people when they suffer, staying with them in every dark valley of shadow and death.

You do not suffer alone. When Jesus died on the cross, he did so alone, bearing the weight of God's wrath for our sin, alone. God raised him from the dead and then sent us the gift of the Holy Spirit after Jesus ascended to heaven. If you are a believer in Christ, the Spirit lives within you. By default, you are never alone, and you certainly never suffer alone. You don't even pray alone. The Holy Spirit intercedes for you when all you can do is sit in sorrow or pain and cry out, "Help me!" (see Rom. 8:26–27).

Take heart that God not only sees your suffering—he is with you in it. You may not ever understand why he has allowed your trials, but you can know that he doesn't waste anything and will prove himself faithful no matter what. Turning your eyes to his word in your pain will help you know for certain that he is with you. And if that's not enough, he's also given you the church to help you press on.

When my son turned ten, we received news from a specialist that a problem with his spine we had been monitoring was growing significantly worse and needed invasive, long-term treatment. After spending six hours at the children's hospital with my son, I tried to hold it together on the long drive home so he wouldn't know I was afraid. All I wanted to do when we finally made it home was to put on some pajama pants, curl up on the couch, and have a good cry. I didn't count on it being a Wednesday and needing to attend church that evening.

Everything in me cried out for some wagon-circling at home. Everyone would have understood if I'd stayed home. But I remembered Paul's call to weep with those who are weeping. How could my church family carry out that command if I didn't *tell* them I was weeping? I went. I shared. I wept. My church family gathered around us, laid hands on us, prayed over us, and wept with us. I was not guaranteed that their prayers would result in my son's healing, but they certainly would result in God's grace to us in this trial. A corner of that huge burden I carried into the church was lifted from my shoulders. Of course, later I went home, put on pajamas, curled up on the couch, and had a good cry. But I did so with hope because I knew I was not alone in the uphill battle before us.

With eyes swollen by tears, I lay awake that night thinking of Moses during the battle of the Amalekites in Exodus 17. As long as he held up his hands, the Israelites were winning the battle. When they dropped, the Amalekites began to succeed. No one can hold up his arms overhead for very long, so when it became apparent that Israel would lose the battle because of Moses's physical weakness, Aaron and Hur stepped in to hold up his arms for him. The beauty of coming to someone's aid when weakness seems to win shouldn't be lost on us. Within the community of the family of God, we should not only seek to hold up the arms of others in their suffering; we should also be transparent about our weaknesses and let them hold our arms up for us.

Your church is God's gift to you. While physical suffering might prevent you from being physically present, don't be emotionally absent from your people. Strive to be open when you can, strive to be present when you can, and let them minister to you. Through them, you are being loved by God. You can, in turn, pray for those around you who are also suffering. Intercession—praying for others—can help move your gaze from your own painful circumstances to others who are hurting.

It is tempting to draw inward and focus on survival when life is hard. But remember that holding on to Christ *is* survival, and it's how we let perseverance complete its work. Do not abandon your post when pain presses in like a knife or loss pushes hope out of your line of vision. Perhaps you'll have days when it is difficult to imagine getting out of bed, let alone reading your Bible or engaging in focused prayer. Faithfulness to Christ in the middle of your trial might mean filling your ears with the words of the Lord while you rest. Perhaps you'll simply read the verses of Lamentations about God's new morning mercies over and over until you've memorized them. Maybe you'll recite them as you try to quiet your tears at night.

Remember that God is always who he has always been. Your trials and suffering do not cancel out his goodness to you. Though you grieve or hurt or yearn for what you've lost, there is still nothing that can separate you from his love. Not death or life, persecutions or afflictions, not disease or chronic pain, not hostility or broken relationships. Nothing can keep you from his love. He has poured out every spiritual blessing on you even if the physical ones seem lacking (see Rom. 8:31–39; Eph. 1:3). If you've lost physical health, remember he has promised a new, resurrected body that will never break down with pain again (see 1 Cor. 15:42–49). If you're grieving a loved one's death, know that, ultimately, Christ has defeated death (see Acts 2:24).

In my experience with physical suffering, drawing near to the Lord when everything hurts can be one of the sweetest ways you will ever grow in godliness. There are some things in life that we cannot learn without having walked through sorrow. Being certain of God's nearness in suffering is one of them. Believe Peter when he says:

> [We] are being guarded through faith for a salvation ready to be revealed in the last time. In this you rejoice, though now for a little while, if necessary, you have been grieved by various trials, so that the tested genuineness of your faith—more precious than gold that perishes though it is tested by fire—may be found to result in praise and glory and honor at the revelation of Jesus Christ. (1 Pet. 1:5–7)

Hold on, friend. The glory is coming. And God himself is invested in your restoration "after you have suffered a little while" (1 Pet. 5:10).

Faithful Like Brooke

I met Brooke when she was in the middle of treatment for stage four breast cancer. Diagnosed in her thirties, Brooke has exemplified perseverance in suffering like no one else I know. Even while enduring multiple discouraging scans, days spent in treatment away from her family, losing her hair, and undergoing surgery, Brooke persistently called attention to God's faithfulness.

Whether through sharing hymns or scriptures or her own words of faith in God's goodness, Brooke fought hard to hold fast to Christ, and everyone knew it. No matter how discouraged she was—and she often was—Brooke lifted her eyes to God's faithful character in his word and reflected his image in her white-knuckled grip on him. Anyone who knows Brooke can see that her strength comes from Christ, for it is an unearthly hope she holds on to.

Brooke has fed her faithfulness during suffering by soaking herself in Scripture, in fellowship with the church, and in prayer. She didn't know that while undergoing her third round of chemo, her physical suffering would be paired with the sudden loss of her husband in a cycling accident. The grief of losing a spouse under any circumstance is earth-shattering. Losing a spouse when you are fighting for your life with three children at home is unfathomable.

Like Job, Brooke has grieved her monumental losses. And, like Job, Brooke reflects on God's character and finds strength in the anchor for her hope. I've watched Brooke rise from the ashes of grief and hold fast to a hope that cannot be taken by cancer, death, or any earthly sorrow. Because her default response to previous suffering was one of Scripture and prayer, her response to her husband's tragic death was the same. She soaked her life with Scripture and prayer. It was all mingled with an ocean of tears, no doubt, but Christ, her steady anchor, never wavered.

I've seen Christians become bitter in their suffering, rejecting the notion that God might still be good. And then I've watched Brooke suffer as one whose hope is built on nothing less than Jesus's blood and righteousness. It is possible to lose nearly everything and still praise the name of the Lord. When Christ is your hope, your faith can flower and grow in life's deepest pain.

7

Faithful When Your Heart Is Cold

My husband and I moved to our farming community during an exceptionally hot, dry summer. The area farmers spent more time irrigating their fields than usual, and we were under a burn ban for most of that summer. One farmer friend gave us a tour of his land, and I was amazed at the effort it took to keep his rice fields under water during a drought. Before that dusty tractor ride, I had no idea that rice must be submerged in water to grow.

I'd never given much thought to the scarcity of rain before as my life has never revolved around growing a food source or making my living from it. While the folks in our community watched the sky like Elijah for rain clouds, I observed the ways the farmers fought for growth when it seemed unlikely. The dirt tractor paths around the fields were parched. But the fields grew heartily beneath the summer sun because the farmers persevered in watering them.

Sometimes my heart feels more like the tractor path than the fields. Dry, dusty, parched. Worn down by rote circling. I can't conjure up any emotion or affection for the Lord. My

Bible reading feels dull. Prayer seems like a fruitless, one-sided conversation that doesn't reach the ceiling, let alone the ears of God. And the front pew on the left side of the church sanctuary is the *last* place I want to be on a Sunday morning.

If you've experienced this before, then you likely know this is commonly called a spiritual dry spell. Seeming to produce little more than apathy, these dry times can pose a serious challenge to growth and steadfastness in faith. Yet the spiritual dry spell doesn't have to be a season when our faithfulness to Jesus shrivels up in drought. When you have to water the fields more than usual, the harvest may yield an abundance of growth.

Obey When You Don't Feel Like It

Many years before he was martyred as a missionary, Jim Elliot wrote in his journal about spiritual dryness: "The Lord has been distant most of this week, and I have found myself too weary and sinful to draw near to him. Desire seemed to fail and my soul lies faint, lapping at its own stale dregs."[1] I find it comforting to know that a man who burned so brightly for Christ experienced periods of soul weariness and apathetic affections just as I have. If you continue reading Elliot's journals, you find that he vacillated between apathy and affection like most of us do, and he had trouble pinpointing just what clouded his heart with stagnant feelings. One of the problems with spiritual dry spells is that you can't forecast their arrival or their departure. You can only irrigate the fields as you watch and wait for rain.

Spiritual dry spells are also problematic because they're usually accompanied by the temptation to abandon the work of daily perseverance altogether. That's what makes them so

---

1. Elisabeth Elliot, *Shadow of the Almighty: The Life and Testament of Jim Elliot* (New York: HarperCollins, 1958), 124.

discouraging—if nothing seems to penetrate the emptiness you're feeling, then what's the point? What's the use of Bible-reading if you're not absorbing anything? Why pray when you know your heart isn't in it? Why take up space on a pew when you feel like you're going through the motions of worship?

It might seem like the right answer is to take a break until you feel a spark of emotion. But when your heart lacks affection toward the Lord, following its direction isn't wise. Our hearts are deceitful and often don't tell us what we need to hear (see Jer. 17:9). It is more likely that abandoning our spiritual disciplines will extend our season of disaffection rather than shorten it. Disengaging isn't the right answer. Obedience is.

Have you noticed that when you're struggling to engage in your individual expressions of faithfulness, you're also resistant to any involvement in church, too? Or, if you've faded from church involvement, your spiritual disciplines have also suffered? Spiritual dryness touches every part of life, and the effects can discourage you from partaking in anything that ordinarily feeds your faithfulness. If you've built your days around following Jesus, then a weary, sluggish spiritual state will affect every part of your life. You might find yourself in quite a vicious cycle of apathy! If you're feeling unmotivated to read your Bible or pray, you might also discover you're hesitant to attend church and be around others who seem to be thriving and growing when you feel stuck in a rut. You might wonder if you should replace those dusty habits of Bible-reading and prayer with other things. Can't a walk in the woods or a weekend at the lake stir up your affections for the Lord more than a whole morning listening to a sermon and singing songs that don't draw out any new emotion? Or maybe you just need a *different* church setting—something to change things up a bit.

What if you don't need something new? What if you need something old? Those everyday expressions of faithfulness that you may want to abandon when they are stripped of emotion or desire are what you need to hold on to during a dry spell. Spiritual disciplines (both individual and corporate) might seem pointless and rote during a spiritual dry spell, but they are key to perseverance through such a time. And they are commanded in Scripture. As we discussed in chapter 2, God ordained the means by which we'll stay close to him. From Hebrews 10 we learned that drawing near, holding fast to our confession, and loving the church will always be the primary ways that we abide in Christ. When you don't want to reach for your Bible, pray, or attend church—do it anyway. These God-ordained means of growth are what you need the most when your heart is cold. God knew what was best for our spiritual growth in giving us these methods of abiding in him.

Think of Asaph's colorful confession in Psalm 73: "I was brutish and ignorant; / I was like a beast toward you" (Ps. 73:22). Not mincing words, he described the way he acted toward the Lord, but then remembered that though he was weak, the Lord was steadfast and continually faithful.

> Nevertheless, I am continually with you;
>   you hold my right hand.
> You guide me with your counsel,
>   and afterward you will receive me to glory.
> Whom have I in heaven but you?
>   And there is nothing on earth that I desire
>   besides you.
> My flesh and my heart may fail,
>   but God is the strength of my heart and my portion
>   forever. (Ps. 73:23–26)

Though his heart was brutish and ignorant, the Lord's counsel and presence revived Asaph's desire for him.

Trusting God with these continued expressions of faithfulness are ordinary ways that we walk by faith and not by sight. It's an exercise of faith in God's wise sovereignty to obey him by abiding in the ways he's given us when our hearts are clogged with discouragement. Stagnant faith may feel like the bigger problem, but abandoning our everyday faithfulness is the real threat here. Stagnant faith that's struggling but pressing on anyway is still faith. And you might look back one day and see that it wasn't stagnant faith at all, but rather a time when the Lord taught you perseverance. If persevering is hard, if it's rote, if it feels like the last thing you want to do, press on. If you're weary, if you're tired, if all your efforts feel in vain, press on. This isn't the time to take a sabbatical until you feel better. It's time to go on the offense.

Make War on Your Dry Spell

God has given us the weapons we need to do battle in this life. If *war* seems like a strong word for this, take note of Paul's exhortations at the end of Ephesians: "Therefore take up the whole armor of God, that you may be able to withstand in the evil day, and having done all, to stand firm" (Eph. 6:13). Paul continues with head-to-toe instructions for suiting up with the truths of Scripture, the gospel of peace, and the shield of faith to stand firm against the spiritual forces of evil we can't see with our physical eyes. What feels like a little spell of apathy might be one of the enemy's fiery darts. If he thinks he can convince you that your faithfulness is doomed by blight and famine, he *will* try. So ready yourself for war with what God has given us to stand firm and persevere. As my husband says to our church when it comes to fighting sin and discouragement:

"Shields up!" Faithfulness is your shield, and God's word is your sword (see Eph. 6:16–17).

Talk of warfare in a chapter on dry spells seems strange, I know. Spiritually dry seasons seem innocuous at first glance—you're just feeling a little off, right?—yet they are opportunities to make war on the desires of the flesh. Instead of pulling back and letting your heart call the shots, press forward *despite* your heart's desire to disengage. Paul encourages us in Galatians to walk in the Spirit so that we don't satisfy the desires of our flesh (see Gal. 5:16–17). The desires of our sinful flesh are diametrically opposed to those of the Spirit who lives in us, so we must always be on guard to live in obedience when our flesh pulls us in the opposite direction of the Lord's commands. This is true even—and especially when—we can't conjure up an enthusiastic desire to obey.

Perseverance Begets Perseverance

We sometimes have the idea that routine obedience is distasteful, that obedience should always be done with loads of enthusiasm. But with time, routine obedience can be a conduit for wholehearted obedience. Sometimes you obey simply because it's disobedience *not* to obey! You pick up your Bible and flood your heart with the words of the Lord because of obedience. You pray not because you always want to, but because God says to draw near. Sometimes you drive to church against an overwhelming desire to stay home because the Lord says not to neglect the body of Christ. You do these things to obey Christ, not because you're always excited to do them. Jesus says that if we love him, we'll obey his commandments (see John 14:15). Abiding in him is done through *obeying* him.

Obedience to Christ's commands may not always begin with joy, but it will end with joy. Jesus said, "These things I have spoken to you, that my joy may be in you, and that your joy may be full" (John 15:11). Obedience to Jesus will keep you by his side, even when your heart is cold. Because it's *Jesus*, the one whose death gave us life! Abiding in him will be too much for your apathy, and you will be filled with joy again. This, friend, is perseverance having its full effect (see James 1:4). We persevere in the face of trials, even if the trial is a cold, unfeeling heart. Apathetic heart? Draw near anyway. Dull, dry Bible reading? Hold on to your confession anyway. No desire to go to church? Meet with your local body of Christ anyway.

Obedience will feed your faithfulness, and perseverance will have its blessed effect in you.

To use King James English, perseverance will *beget* perseverance. Your steadfastness will grow when you practice it, though everything in you resists. You'll train your heart to default to single-minded obedience no matter how you feel about it. This isn't distasteful; this is beautiful. This is maturity. This is everyday faithfulness. When obedience becomes more and more a default response, you will be well equipped to press forward when your heart feels like it's lagging several steps behind you. Joy will return (see Ps. 30:5)—maybe not on your timetable, but it will return. In the meantime, you'll be watering the field of your faithfulness while you watch and wait for rain.

Slow Growth for a Long Game

It can be difficult to imagine staking our lives—for the rest of our lives—on a mission of everyday, regular faithful plodding. We want exciting results that are both encouraging to our perseverance and visible to the world around us because we want the world to see that Jesus is glorious! The slowness of faithfulness and spiritual growth might make us question if we're "doing it right." Bumping up against a fight with apathy exacerbates the problem. However, though the returns of everyday, ordinary plodding are often slow in coming, they have eternal, immeasurable longevity. As Paul said to Timothy, "Train yourself for godliness; for . . . godliness is of value in every way, since it holds promise for the present life and also for the life to come" (1 Tim. 4:7–8). We know our life to come will be eternal, so training ourselves for godliness produces some *very* long-term benefits.

The challenge here is patience. Slow returns quickly derail us. We want every attempt at Bible study or prayer to be more memorable and meaningful than the last. We measure growth with emotion rather than commitment. So when faced with a string of days in a challenging section of the Bible or a week of prayer that feels fruitless, we quit. Trevin Wax helps us understand why we should press through anyway:

> Change doesn't always happen overnight. Growth doesn't happen in an instant. Instead, it happens over time, as we eat and drink and exercise. The same is true of Scripture reading. Not every meal is at a steakhouse. Not every meal is memorable. Can you remember what you had for dinner, say, two weeks ago? Probably not. But that meal sustained you, didn't it? In the same way, we come to feast on God's Word, recognizing that it's the daily rhythm of submitting ourselves to God and bringing our plans and hopes and fears to Him that makes the difference.[2]

Everyday faithfulness sustains us even if it isn't as memorable as we'd like it to be. If we abandon spiritual disciplines because the work of plodding seems daunting, boring, or too

---

2. Trevin Wax, "Routine Bible Reading Can Change Your Life," *Lifeway Voices*, December 3, 2018, https://lifewayvoices.com/bible-theology/routine-bible-reading-can-change-your-life/.

slow, we miss the joy that comes through perseverance (James 1:4). The apostle Peter helps us understand that our definition of slowness is limited. We are bound by time in a way that God is not: "But do not overlook this one fact, beloved, that with the Lord one day is as a thousand years, and a thousand years as one day. The Lord is not slow to fulfill his promise as some count slowness, but is patient toward you, not wishing that any should perish, but that all should reach repentance" (2 Pet. 3:8–9). Referring to the return of Christ, Peter explains that what seems slow in coming to us is not slow in the grand scheme of God's sovereign plan.

Your plodding may feel every bit like plodding. Or maybe it's slower than that—maybe it's more like crawling—army-crawling with bloody knees and a weary soul. Even so, that's still perseverance. John Calvin encouraged believers not to be discouraged by what appears to be slow or little growth. Growth is still growth. Calvin encourages us: "None of us will move forward with so little success that we will not make some daily progress in the way. Therefore, let us keep trying so that we might continually make some gains in the way of the Lord, and neither let us despair over how small our successes are."[3]

We can press forward in faithfulness knowing that trials come and go, but Jesus is our sure and steady anchor. Fixing our eyes on him helps us to move forward, even when the moving seems slow. The author of Hebrews exhorts us to "lay aside every weight, and sin which clings so closely, and let us run with endurance the race that is set before us, looking to Jesus, the founder and perfecter of our faith, who for the joy that was set before him endured the cross, despising the shame, and is seated at the right hand of the throne of God" (Heb. 12:1–2). When our hearts feel cold, when the field is parched, when

---

3. A. Denlinger and B. Parsons, *A Little Book on the Christian Life* (Orlando, FL: Reformation Trust, 2017), 16.

the rote patterns of discipline seem absolutely meaningless, the cure is found in looking at Jesus. Again. And again. And again. As author Jared C. Wilson explains, "Beholding Christ's glory is the number-one directive for following Jesus. And, in fact, it's sometimes the only effort we lousy disciples can muster up."[4] The solution for the spiritual dry spell will always be to look at Jesus.

Practically Speaking

When I say we must look at Jesus over and over again, I do mean *look at him*. We look to him with our spiritual eyes, beholding him through the means of faithfulness we've been following throughout this book: regular Bible reading, prayer, and connection to the body of Christ. The gifts of communion with God, Scripture, and teaching and oversight from the church are provisions that help us persevere. Sometimes, though, we might need to rethink our approach to them or do things that will renew our commitment to their practice.

First, pray. It's the last thing you want to do when you've been plowing through a dry season. But prayer is when you talk to the Lord about your apathy, your emptiness, your struggle to feel motivated to obey him. Be honest before the Lord, for he knows your heart better than you do. Pray for him to rekindle your affections for him, pray for him to help you persevere when you don't want to, pray for him to help you see his faithfulness to you more clearly. Remember David's prayer: "Restore to me the joy of your salvation, / and uphold me with a willing spirit" (Ps. 51:12). Practice gratitude in your prayer, remembering all the ways God has sustained you thus far. Remember the love God demonstrated in transferring you

---

4. Jared C. Wilson, *The Imperfect Disciple: Grace for People Who Can't Get Their Act Together* (Grand Rapids, MI: Baker, 2017), 70.

from the kingdom of darkness to the kingdom of Christ. Speak those things out loud to the Lord—not because he needs to be reminded, but because you do.

Second, read your Bible. Every day. We do this not to be legalistic but to be *sustained*. You're not checking a box but reminding yourself of what's true. The Bible is no empty word but your very life (see Deut. 32:47). It is not like a novel designed to fill some empty hours. It's not like a newspaper with words that are undermined by time and change. No, the Bible is the living and active word of God, able to separate joint and marrow, soul and spirit (see Heb. 4:12). These are the very useful words of the Lord, written down for us. And because the Spirit lives in you, Christian, you have help to absorb and understand the scriptures when your mind is cloudy with fatigue or your heart is blocked up with apathy. You aren't just skimming a good story. You are watering your soul with the nourishing words of the Lord.

These words were powerful enough to lead you to salvation; they are powerful enough to preserve you through sanctification. So read your Bible. Every day. If you're not using any study tools, perhaps choose one of the study questions in chapter 2 and focus on reading the Bible with that one question in mind. For example, read through the book of Ephesians and write down everything you learn about God's character. Or read Colossians and note everything that Christ has done for the believer. Read Leviticus and Hebrews together and list the ways Jesus fulfilled the law so that you can have free access to God. Look at Jesus until you can really see him.

Third, confess your struggles to another believer and stay connected to your church. While it's tempting to find solace in solitude, the impulse to insulate yourself from the world is not from God. You *need* the body of Christ to endure every season of faithfulness. Go to church. Every Sunday. Especially on the weeks you don't feel like it. Share with a pastor or member what you're experiencing, and let them pray for you. Let those who aren't in a dry spell help carry you through yours. Then one day you'll be prepared to do the same for them.

Last, take some extra steps that will feed all of the above encouragements. Take a walk and listen to some good, gospel-rich music to help stir your affections for Christ. I find that songs that tell the gospel story help me to remember what God has done for me in Christ. Sing songs that praise God for his attributes. Music has a way of touching our emotional centers when nothing else does. Take advantage of this and listen to songs that will turn your face to Jesus. Listening to Scripture through an app or audio Bible is another way to get the truth of God's word down into your heart.

Scripture memorization is a key tool for breaking through the tough exterior of a dry heart. Learning the words of the Lord encourages praise (Ps. 119:7). If reading the Bible is like irrigating a field, then memorization is like flooding the field with water to submerge it. Pastor Jon Bloom calls memorization "swimming" in the text rather than just skimming the surface.[5] Through repetition and recitation, the words of the Lord are hidden in our hearts and come to mind throughout the day. When you commit portions of Scripture to memory, you'll find that those passages begin to change the way you think and feel. This is how you flood the fields, my friend.

Beyond the things you can *do* to recapture your desire for spiritual disciplines, also consider what you need to *not do*. Sometimes I find that feeling spiritually sluggish has a direct correlation to the amount of time I spend on Netflix

5. Jon Bloom. "Scripture Memory Wasn't for Me," Desiring God website, April 5, 2019, https://www.desiringgod.org/articles/scripture-memory-wasnt-for-me/.

or social media. There's no space in my head for thinking about the Lord when most of my media consumption turns my face away from him. Take a break from all the input, especially the kind that might be crowding out the true, lovely, praiseworthy things (see Phil. 4:8). Create some space in your head and heart to think about what is *good* for your head and heart. Make an agreement with a friend that you won't touch your phone until you've met with the Lord in the mornings. Put your devices away or turn off all media for an hour before bed. Read, write, pray, rest. These are good practices to help quiet your thoughts and to listen for the still, small voice that we tend to quiet with the kind of noise that doesn't matter all that much.

As you practice your everyday faithfulness, remember that God is with you in it. When you cannot feel him, he's still present because he has given us the gift of the Spirit to live in us, intercede for us, and help us to persevere. Remember that the Bible is no empty word, but our *very life*, and we cannot endure difficult seasons divorced from God's word. Remember to turn your eyes toward Christ. You can trust God to bring about good from your endeavors. He is invested in your plodding. Jesus promised us in John 15:11 that when our love is displayed by obedience to him, we'll have his joy and it will be full. Your dry spell won't last forever, and the Lord can cultivate much fruit from your efforts at faithful plodding.

Near the end of that first dry summer in our community, an elderly church member and his wife took my husband and me out to dinner. As we drove past many fields of brown, dry corn, I remarked that it was a shame the corn crop had been lost by the harsh heat in spite of all the farmers' efforts at irrigation. The older gentlemen laughed and said, "Don't worry. The stalks look dead, but that's when they're ready to harvest. Those fields are full of ripe corn, young lady. The farmers will have a big crop this year!" What seemed dry and wasted wasn't, in fact, dry or wasted. At the end of every summer, I'm reminded that dry spells don't last forever, and they are not for nothing.

Faithful Like Ranelle

Ranelle didn't come to saving faith in Christ until she was in her midforties. Immersed in a healthy local church with sound, biblical teaching, Ranelle built her new life in Christ around the practices of prayer, Bible-reading, discipleship, and church involvement. The first decade of her relationship with Jesus was full of immense growth and passion.

As Ranelle grew older, she faced various trials that challenged her faithfulness: loneliness, depression, undesired singleness, and long bouts of apathy she couldn't explain. The individual and corporate spiritual disciplines that had once fueled her faith became rote and dull. Longing to return to the phase of life when her heart was full of affection for Christ, Ranelle kept pressing forward in the things she knew would one day awaken her heart: Bible-reading, prayer, and church involvement. She kept up her discipleship relationships with younger women, though she felt ill-equipped to do so, and trusted the Lord with the results. She experienced occasional reprieves from her spiritual apathy, yet the dry seasons seemed to normalize and become part of her regular life. She began to meditate on God's word more by memorizing Scripture, reciting passages over and over until they were firmly entrenched in her heart.

Ranelle, like many of us, vacillates between affection and apathy. Her faithfulness may not look glamorous as she continues to live her life around God's word, prayer, and the church, but her daily expressions of faith keep her near the Father's side in seasons of both famine and fruitfulness. Though she may not see the growth, it is evident to those around her who watch her plod forward in quiet, everyday faithfulness.

8

Faithful When You Sin

It's an oxymoron to title a chapter "Faithful When You Sin," right? To link the words *faithful* and *sin* seems a misunderstanding of . . . well, *everything* about the gospel. When we give in to temptation and find ourselves guiltily recovering from a sinful display of anger, selfishness, gossip, lust, or pride, surely we are sitting squarely opposite of everyday faithfulness. We've established that faithfulness means following Christ steadfastly no matter what season or difficulty we face in life. So, where does our struggle with sin factor into our perseverance? If we can persevere through suffering, doubt, and deferred hopes, can we also continue walking as sinful people in faithfulness to and with Jesus?

No one who has followed Christ faithfully has ever done so perfectly. The most sainted, well-read, devout, theological giant you can think of has failed the Lord repeatedly. Daily, hourly. Yet we know faithful believers whose lives are undoubtedly marked by persevering faith in spite of their daily fight with sin. The key here is found in that last sentence. Faithful believers *fight* their sin. And this commitment to fight sin is a mark of true, saving faith. Those who have been made new in Christ will regularly seek to put their sin to death, and though they will not do it perfectly, they will grow in maturity as they are sanctified and made more and more into the image of Jesus.

Faithfulness is not found in living perfectly but in killing sin regularly.

In this chapter, we'll discuss why fighting our sin is important, how to continue in everyday faithfulness after we've sinned, and how our daily expressions of faith help us in our fight against temptation. We will also look at some practical steps for putting our sin to death, and while some of them may seem extreme or costly, they will aid in our fight for faithfulness.

Celebrating a Funeral

Many years ago, a friend of mine came to faith in Christ after a decade of addiction and marital unfaithfulness. I remember the first time I saw him after his profession of faith. He looked *different*. He was himself, and yet somehow not himself. He was a new version of my formerly dead friend. His old self had been crucified with Christ, and his life as a new creation in Christ filled him with joy.

As discussed in chapter 5, when we have been made alive in Christ, we are completely new creations. We are not who we used to be. Once slaves, now we're free. Once God's enemies, now we're his children. Once dead in our sins, now we're alive in Christ. Once alienated, now we're reconciled. Once part of the domain of darkness, now we're members of the kingdom of the Son. Those old versions of ourselves are corpses that have been buried with Christ in death and raised in newness of life (see Rom. 6:4). And though we still face temptation, we are now free *not* to sin.

Before Christ, we obeyed our sinful hearts at every turn. But in Christ, we are free to fight our sin instead of serving it. The apostle Paul tells us in Romans that "the law of the Spirit of life has set you free in Christ Jesus from the law of sin and death" (Rom. 8:2). Since we don't live according to our flesh anymore, we no longer obey the flesh or think the way that our pre-redeemed minds thought: "You, however, are not in the flesh but in the Spirit, if in fact the Spirit of God dwells in you. . . . But if Christ is in you, although the body is dead because of sin, the Spirit is life because of righteousness" (Rom. 8:9–10). We don't serve and obey a corpse. We serve and obey the Spirit of God who now lives in us. Our effort at killing our sin is evidence that the Spirit truly does live within us.

John Piper describes how we can speak to our old self when we are tempted to sin. He encourages us to talk to our old selves and say, "I deny you! You're dead!"[1] My old self, the one that raged against God, the one that happily opposed God in hostility with a darkened heart, the one that only wanted to serve herself—that old me is dead and buried. So I can deny her the indulgences she demands. When she lights a match in anger, I don't have to warm myself at her fire. When she stands at the pantry or the fridge seeking comfort after a tough day, I don't have to swallow her poor substitutions for peace. When she remembers an unkind comment someone made, I don't have to share it with a friend. When she despairs of overcoming any of those temptations, I can remember that Jesus has given me victory over sin.

That old me doesn't rule me anymore. Jesus died for her and paid for her desperate wretchedness at the cross. And since God resurrected Jesus from the grave, I know that the old me will stay dead and the new me will live because of Christ. "I

---

1. John Piper, "Unashamed to Be Scorned with Jesus" (sermon, TGC National Conference, Indianapolis, IN, April 1, 2019).

have been crucified with Christ. It is no longer I who live, but Christ who lives in me. And the life I now live in the flesh I live by faith in the Son of God, who loved me and gave himself for me" (Gal. 2:20). I deny my old self—she's dead! And because she has been dethroned in my heart by Christ himself, I *can* fight my sin. I must fight it.

This old/new and flesh/Spirit language is peppered throughout much of Paul's writings in the New Testament. Since we're prone to downplaying our sin, we'll always need Paul's reminders to fight it. Fight it to the death, actually. Paul says:

> Put to death therefore what is earthly in you: sexual im-morality, impurity, passion, evil desire, and covetousness, which is idolatry. On account of these the wrath of God is coming. In these you too once walked, when you were liv-ing in them. But now you must put them all away: anger, wrath, malice, slander, and obscene talk from your mouth. Do not lie to one another, seeing that you have put off the old self with its practices and have put on the new self, which is being renewed in knowledge after the image of its creator. (Col. 3:5–10)

This putting off and putting on are the actions of faith-fulness, of aligning your lifestyle with your new identity in Christ, of being who you now really are. When we forget who we are in Christ and give in to temptation, we may feel we're losing the fight. But the fighting itself is what cultivates per-severance and proves we are truly *in* Christ.

If you're reading this and beginning to feel a tremor of doubt (especially if you have a scrupulous conscience), go back to chapter 5 and remind yourself that the ability to fight sin is anchored in the redeeming work of Christ. If God has saved you, he *will* sanctify you. Remember that he is invested in your perseverance! His Spirit within you enables you to deny your old self and live as a new creation in Christ. You are not fighting alone.

Eye-Gouging and Amputations

The biblical commands to put sin to death are wrapped in action. They require diligence and preparedness, never encouraging us to be passive or merely reactionary. We cannot sit in the comfortable bunkers of our twenty-first-century existence and pass through life waiting for something to happen before we scramble to arm ourselves with protection. The New Testament writers give exhortations and commands that conjure up preemptive and aggressive imagery rather than reactionary. Peter warns us to "be watchful. Your adversary the devil prowls around like a roaring lion, seeking someone to devour" (1 Pet. 5:8). If Satan isn't passive, we certainly shouldn't be either. He's working hard to convince us that we're still wearing chains, that we'll never have victory over sin, that we're every bit of our old selves who loved hostility toward God. Satan wants us to believe that sin is sweet and satisfying, that God may not be trustworthy, and that obedience is legalistic. To stand firm in gospel victory, we must prepare for Satan's attacks *before* he comes at us with lies.

In his Sermon on the Mount, Jesus addresses sins that begin internally (anger and lust) and equates them with external expressions of those sins (murder and adultery; Matt. 5:21–30). Jesus exposes sin that can lead to more sin with wider repercussions. Jesus uses some harsh words here! I'm certain he had everyone's attention when he said that "if your right eye causes you to sin, tear it out and throw it away" and "if your right hand causes you to sin, cut it off and throw it away" (Matt. 5:29–30). Jesus isn't actually advocating for self-mutilation, but he is telling us to remove from ourselves the things that regularly cause us to sin, no matter how painful or radical it may feel. Faithfulness to Christ in fighting sin means that we do not linger near places, things, or circumstances that generate temptation to obey our old desires. Active, preemptive sin-killing cuts the things out of your life that entice you to disobey God.

We'll get into specifics later, but this eye-gouging and hand-amputating Jesus speaks of implies taking drastic, life-altering measures to safeguard yourself from areas of sin to which you are especially prone. Don Carson says we must "deal drastically with sin. We must not pamper it, flirt with it, enjoy nibbling a little of it around the edges. We are to hate it, crush it, dig it out."[2] Playing with sin will lead us down a path we will regret. Jesus plainly tells us why: "For it is better that you lose one of your members than that your whole body be thrown into hell" (Matt. 5:29). Better to block the paths to sin than to follow them to unfaithfulness.

To persevere in fighting sin, we must take up our weapons and aggressively do battle. Rather than waiting for sin to overtake us before we jump up to fight, we must stand firm with the truth of the gospel in the power of the Spirit *before* temptation befalls us. Ever ready, we must hold our ground before the devil's schemes whistle over our bunker and blow us to bits. Everyday faithfulness is ready for battle, and it will do what it takes to stand firm. Perseverance will not set up camp in places with weak defenses. Steadfastness will ensure that the enemy doesn't creep up unexpected. We fight

2. D. A. Carson, *Jesus' Sermon on the Mount and His Confrontation with the World* (Grand Rapids, MI: Global Christian Publishers, 2001), 47.

preemptively, preparing for temptation before it starts and building safeguards into our everyday living to strengthen our defense.

Prepare Like Jesus

The story of Jesus's temptation in the wilderness in Matthew 4 helps us understand how to prepare to stand firm against the devil's attacks. Jesus was physically weak from fasting when Satan showed up to prey on that weakness. Satan struck at Jesus's hunger, his identity, and his obedience to the Father. Coming at Jesus with a balm for his physical needs, a quick path to a kingdom, and a change in loyalties, Satan had clearly planned for this. He was scheming, looking to devour the faithfulness of the Messiah himself.

Jesus was prepared, however. And not just because he was God in the flesh. He was prepared with the words of Scripture as his defense. Jesus didn't have just a slight grasp on the truth of God's word. The word was a sword he knew how to wield when faced with temptation. His responses to Satan revealed not just knowledge of Scripture but an ownership of them that gave him the way out. And that is the gift we also have when Satan tries to rouse our old, dead selves with the things we used to worship. God will always provide a way out. What a mercy! Though we're not invincible, we have a great Savior who resisted temptation with the help of the same Spirit who lives in us. Charles Spurgeon wrote:

> Christ is not a Savior for some things, but for all things. He does not come in to help his people only on certain days and only under certain assaults. He comes to their rescue in all temptations and in all trials. Weak as you are, he can strengthen you. Fierce though the temptation may be, he

can cover you from head to foot with a full suit of armor in which you will stand gloriously clothed.[3]

In the beginning of 1 Corinthians 10 Paul says that the stories of sin and judgment of the Old Testament should teach us that there are grave consequences for our sin. He then warns: "Therefore let anyone who thinks that he stands take heed lest he fall" (1 Cor. 10:12). Take heed—prepare and be watchful. But we should also be encouraged, for "no temptation has overtaken you that is not common to man. God is faithful, and he will not let you be tempted beyond your ability, but with the temptation he will also provide a way of escape, that you may be able to endure it" (1 Cor. 10:13). When we are teetering on the edge of faithfulness, God is faithful to provide a way out. He is invested in our fight against sin!

Jen Wilkin writes, "Take note that God provides the way of escape in faithfulness. Even as we contemplate unfaithfulness to him, he stands faithfully pointing the way to salvation."[4] We can be confident that God will always give us a way out. Sometimes that will look like gouging out your eye, and sometimes it will look like cutting off your hand, and always it will look like standing firm on Scripture as you wage war against the desires of your old self.

Faithfulness after Failure

But what about the times you willfully give in to temptation? You've chosen to do something you know is wrong, something you weren't prepared (or didn't want) to fight, something you're afraid you'll never overcome. You wrestled with it for a while before giving in, or maybe it was a split-second

3. Charles Spurgeon, *God's Gift to You* (New Kensington, PA: Whitaker House, 1997), 196.

4. Jen Wilkin, *In His Image: 10 Ways God Calls Us to Reflect His Character* (Wheaton, IL: Crossway, 2018), 103.

decision you made. Regardless of whether your decision was premeditated or not, regardless of how you did or didn't want to resist, here you are shrouded in a cloak of guilt and exhaling apologies thick with shame to the Lord. Self-loathing settles in along with the vows to never participate in this behavior again.

How do we continue in faithfulness after we've sinned? We know we won't obey perfectly this side of heaven, and though we grow in spiritual maturity, we often lose our fight with sin. Can faithfulness be resumed or are we doomed to repeat our mistakes over and over again? What keeps us moving forward in our sanctification when it feels like we're moving backward?

After you've sinned, the path to faithfulness is paved with repentance. And by *repentance*, I mean confessing your sin to God with real grief and turning your face back toward Christ rather than toward your sin again. Repentance acknowledges that we have disobeyed God and loved him less than our desires. Repentance concedes our idolatry, names it, and seeks to flee far from it. Repentance seeks forgiveness from God and asks him for strength to believe we really have it. Repentance remembers the gospel and the freedom Christ won for us at the cross. Repentance turns our face toward Jesus instead of the vile temptations of sin and self. Repentance is how we continue in everyday faithfulness, free from condemnation and judgment. Peter said to "repent therefore, and turn back, that your sins may be blotted out, that times of refreshing may come from the presence of the Lord" (Acts 3:19–20).

Continual, unrepentant sin is often a sign of unbelief; those who truly follow Christ do not make a habit of their sin. They practice righteousness instead:

Whoever practices righteousness is righteous, as he is righteous. Whoever makes a practice of sinning is of the devil, for the devil has been sinning from the beginning. . . . No one born of God makes a practice of sinning, for God's seed abides in him; and he cannot keep on sinning, because he has been born of God. By this it is evident who are the children of God, and who are the children of the devil: whoever does not practice righteousness is not of God, nor is the one who does not love his brother. (1 John 3:7–10)

The regular act of repentance and turning our faces away from sin and toward the Lord is how we practice righteousness. Those who practice sin are not concerned with where their faces are turned.

Turning back to the Lord means we don't have to dwell on our past sin, whether it's sin from twenty years ago or twenty minutes ago. The Lord's forgiveness covers the widest berth. He neither remembers nor holds it against those who are in him (see Ps. 103:11–12; Heb. 8:12). Following our confession and repentance, we can be refreshed by the forgiveness of a gracious and merciful God. Repentance should lead us to worship and praise! Though we do not want to presume upon God's kindness and mercy (for so doing minimizes his holiness and Jesus's sacrifice on the cross), we can be confident that he will be faithful when we are unfaithful (2 Tim. 2:13). As one of my favorite hymns says, "Our sins, they are many, his mercy is more."[5] And if we truly believe that his mercy is bigger than our vilest offenses, then we will practice righteousness to make much of that mercy. We will pit ourselves against our sins and loathe them with all our heart.

---

5. Matt Boswell and Matt Papa, "His Mercy Is More," © 2016 Getty Music Songs and Hymns (ASCAP), Love Your Enemies Publishing (ASCAP), Getty Music Publishing (BMI), and Messenger Hymns (BMI) (all adm. by MusicService.org).

Practically Speaking

Everyday faithfulness does not have to be strangled by sin. We can set safeguards in our life to protect us from future temptation, and we can continue in victory in the war against our sin even if we've failed to win a battle against it. Perseverance looks like both the avoidance of sin *and* pursuing more love for Christ. It's looking away from disobedience and toward Christ. It's denying ourselves what gives brief pleasure but long-term destruction and instead loving what God loves. As John Calvin reminds us, "You won't find any proper remedy to such vices other than to deny yourself, to disregard your own ambitions, and to stretch your mind to seek wholly those things that the Lord requires of you—and to seek them because they are pleasing to him."[6]

How do we avoid sin and love God more? We avoid sin *by* loving God more. God has given us more than a list of "thou shalt nots." His word contains immense riches that lead us to set our affections upon the gloriousness of our God. We take advantage of the same spiritual disciplines that help us persevere through our doubts, dryspells, busy seasons, and afflictions to kindle our affections for God and wither our desire for sin. We flee sin by drawing near to God. Every day. Because every day we forget that God is more glorious than our sin. As Pastor Stephen Whitmer writes, "Even after conversion, Jesus's followers all too frequently struggle to see God as glorious and desirable, and to orient our lives fully toward him. We're tempted every day in a thousand different directions. Therefore, we must constantly reorient ourselves back toward God, seeing him anew and pursuing him afresh."[7]

---

6. A. Denlinger and B. Parson, eds., *A Little Book on the Christian Life* (Orlando, FL: Reformation Trust, 2017), 27.

7. Stephen Whitmer, "Unless You Stop Loving Sin: The Heart of Repentance," Desiring God website, February 24, 2019, https://www.desiringgod.org/articles/unless-you-stop-loving-sin/.

This reorientation comes as a result of soaking our lives in Scripture, in prayer, and in meeting with other believers to hear the word proclaimed. The rhythms of grace that keep us close to the Father's side also keep us far from sin. They help us to see that God is more satisfying than anything else we could pursue. We are less likely to wander into sinful indulgence when we are centering our hearts and minds on the Father's will each day.

The practices of prayer, Bible reading, and meeting together with our church hold out both the gloriousness of God to us as well as gospel hope. Through them, we see that God is more satisfying than our sinful desires and that there is hope for restoration when we fail to believe that truth. Drawing near to the Lord regularly helps us to see sin as it is and to hate it. Puritan pastor Thomas Watson said that "a true penitent is a sin-loather," and "Christ is never loved—until sin is loathed."[8] Hatred of sin can be expressed in the ways that we safeguard our lives from it. This takes us back to Jesus's shocking exhortation in Matthew 5 to gouge out our eyes or cut off our hands. Loathing sin means cutting off any path to it from our lives.

If watching shows on Netflix leads you to sin, either because of immoral content or the amount of time you devote to watching, then cancel Netflix. If impulsive shopping is a temptation, talk to your spouse or a trusted friend about monitoring your spending habits as you pray and seek the Lord about what you're trying to accomplish with material things. If gossip is a real temptation, do not put yourself in situations that invite you to do speak ill of others. Don't live your life in places that encourage you to indulge in sin. Step far away from the perimeters of temptation where you're particularly weak.

---

8. Thomas Watson, *The Doctrine of Repentance* (1668; CreateSpace Independent Publishing Platform, August 17, 2015), 20.

I once had to cut an entire genre of music from my life because listening to it led my mind to wander to unsafe places. It was a painful cut because I am a musician, but that particular brand of music discouraged my faithfulness to Christ and tempted me with sinful thoughts. I had to gouge out my eye to keep on the path of faithfulness. Even small actions of everyday faithfulness will cost us something. Yet the rewards of nearness to Christ are immeasurably more valuable than anything we must remove. Though painful at first, you'll find great relief in unburdening yourself from the things that lead you to sin. It is a sweet consolation to find that you can't access the paths to temptation because you've cut off all the entrances.

Drawing near to the Lord through prayer, reading his word, and meeting with believers helps not only to avoid temptation but also to fill our minds and time with things that are uplifting and will encourage our faithfulness. Paul says to think on things that are true, honorable, just, pure, lovely, commendable, excellent, and praiseworthy (see Phil. 4:8). *Do* live your life in places that support and strengthen your fight against sin.

I can't underscore enough how vital the church is in the Christian's fight against sin. I have found small midweek prayer meetings and Bible study groups to be good settings for transparency and confession. Meeting with an accountability partner or group can build regular routines of confession and prayer into your life. Speaking our struggles out loud somehow helps to loosen their grip on us. When the sin we've hidden in the darkness is brought out into the light, we find it loses its power. And we are less likely to willfully dabble in these areas when our church is invested in our fight against sin.

If the idea of accountability is new for you, pray and ask one of your pastors about finding someone in your church who could meet with you weekly for accountability.[9] Look for a partner who will hold you accountable while also holding out the hope of the gospel to you. Think of this as both a way to resume faithfulness after you've sinned and to preemptively prepare for future temptation.

Take a long view of your fight with sin. Like the other obstacles to everyday faithfulness we've discussed so far, victory doesn't often happen overnight. Start making war on your sin now so you can have victory over it later. Jesus is worth it, friend. He is more glorious and more satisfying than any poor, earthly substitution.

---

9. In light of Titus 2, it is wise for women to meet with other women and men to meet with other men. The private nature of some sins makes a same-gender accountability relationship essential.

Faithful Like Dora

Dora became a believer when she was eighteen. Because she wasn't raised in a Christian environment, following Jesus involved radical changes as she moved from sinner to saint. Now a wife, mother of two, and nurse, Dora's life revolves around Bible study, prayer, and church involvement.

I met Dora at church, and her honest conversations about her relationship with Jesus drew me to her instantly. Dora's transparency about her sin, her love for Christ, her concern for the spiritual welfare of her coworkers, and her regular witness to God's goodness exhibit what everyday faithfulness looks like in the average Christ follower.

As she's grown in spiritual maturity, Dora has seen the value of waging war against her sin. She shared with me once that it has taken much of her thirteen years as a believer to kill one area of sin. She'd grown up with this particular sin—it was a normal part of life for her until she heard the gospel and believed it. From that day forward, it was clear that she could worship only one master. To fight her sin, Dora armed herself with Scripture and prayer. She set up habits of accountability, freely confessed to fellow church members, and repented when she failed.

After thirteen years of faithful fighting, Dora has finally found victory over this area of sin. It was a long, difficult fight. Though she surely begged God to make her battle easier, the longevity of her fight cultivated perseverance that encouraged her faithfulness in other areas. Her commitment to God's word, prayer, and the church causes her stand to out at work, where she strives to speak the gospel often. Her coworkers may not understand why she has taken such drastic measures to be ruled by Christ rather than her sin, but her everyday faithfulness is remarkable in an ordinary life of work and worship.

9

Faithful to the End

Leota died when she was ninety-six years old. We had met twelve years earlier when she was eighty-four and I was twenty-four, but the six decades between us seemed only a small breath. I invited myself to her house a few weeks after my husband and I settled into the church parsonage in our new small town. She was widowed and had seemed lonely when I met her in the church foyer. The first time I knocked on her front door, Leota welcomed me in with a wide smile. We shared a love of reading and flowers (though she had many years of successful gardening behind her, and I, well, we all know I *didn't*). Each time I visited, she doled out little bits about her life, her marriage, her daughter, and her grandson. She loved to study the Bible and spent hours every evening reading the word. She remarked after nearly every Sunday sermon that she still had much to learn. My visits tapered off after I started a new job and later had children. But I watched my elderly sister in Christ continue to grow in faith even though she'd been doing so for decades longer than I'd been alive.

After she died, I felt her absence keenly. She used to sit behind me on the third pew on the left side of the sanctuary, and no matter how much her arthritis hurt or how ineffectively her hearing aids were working, she was there every single Sunday until a stroke sent her first to a nursing home and then to heaven. Leota was buried a few hours away from our town, and we'd had rough winter weather not long before her funeral. Only a handful of people were present when she was interred. Home with young children, I was heartbroken to miss it.

I thought about the tiny gathering of seven or eight people who stood next to her grave while the earth swallowed her earthly body. Leota wasn't well known or famous. Few people knew or will remember her name. She didn't have a big corporate job or run a nonprofit. She didn't blog or use social media (she didn't even own a computer!). She outlived most of her family and had a small circle of friends from Bible study. She lived a quiet life in a small town. And yet, her regular, everyday faithfulness to Christ has impacted my life more than almost anyone I have ever known. Without accolades, praise, or the knowledge that anyone was watching her, Leota was faithful to the end. I only wish I could have seen her face when she heard the words, "Well done, good and faithful servant" (Matt. 25:21).

Everyday Faithfulness Is for Every Believer

Remarkably unremarkable, Leota is just one of countless saints who have followed Jesus wholeheartedly until he called them home. Most of the names of lifelong faithful believers aren't recorded in history books or occupying space on the shelves of bookstores. The kingdom of God belongs to all kinds of people from every corner of the earth, and most of them lived and will live out their faithfulness in complete anonymity. No matter our background or life circumstances, faithfulness is expected of each of us from day one of our salvation until the end of our sanctification.

Jesus said that "the one who endures to the end will be saved" (Matt. 24:13). Perseverance until the end reveals that our profession of faith was genuine, that we really are children of God, that his investment in our holiness is true. Whether we're headlining a major event, leading from a stage, running a company, teaching classrooms full of children, working at Walmart, or shuffling around our homes in old age, when we have Christ, we have the ability to be faithful to him until he calls us home. In the words of one writer:

> Christianity is a lifelong surrender to Christ. There is no such thing as "retirement" in the kingdom of God, and, therefore, if we are truly in Christ, we will never abandon our callings as members of the one body nor shirk our responsibility to guard the deposit of truth the apostles and prophets have left for us. Even if we can no longer work full-time or are too weak or frail to serve physically, we can pray and encourage others in the fight.[1]

The obstacles to our faithfulness are many—waiting, deferred hopes, busyness, suffering, doubt, temptation. It's helpful to know that these are common obstacles and that many believers have walked the well-worn path of everyday faithfulness before us and encountered the same struggles that we do. God preserved them as they persevered. If I had asked Leota to share her secret to faithful Christ-following, she would have laughed and said something like, "Why, it's nothing fancy. Just read your Bible and pray every day and be involved in church as

---

1. "The Duration of Our Charge," *Tabletalk*, August 25, 2009, https://tabletalk magazine.com/daily-study/2009/08/duration-our-charge/.

much as you can." Even in her nineties, she would have added that she had a long way to go, too, because she just couldn't get enough of Jesus. Her words wouldn't be eloquent or deeply intellectual. Her instructions would have been straightforward and self-deprecating, and completely to the point. Everyday faithfulness doesn't have to be complicated. We keep looking at Jesus because, as theologian D. A. Carson writes:

> We tend to move toward the object on which we fix our gaze. In the same way, our whole lives drift relentlessly toward the spot where our treasures are stored, because our hearts will take us there. To follow Jesus faithfully entails therefore a consistent development of our deepest loves, to train ourselves to adopt an unswerving loyalty to kingdom values and to delight in all that God approves.[2]

This is what it means to set our minds on heavenly things instead of earthly things, even in the most normal, humdrum days of our existence. Keep looking at Jesus. He is our ever-fixed point.

When I'm pressing through seasons of day-in-and-day-out sameness, I like to think of Paul's advice to "live quietly, and to mind your own affairs, and to work with your hands" (1 Thess. 4:11). Perseverance in the faith will often bump up against trials, sin, busy seasons, and longings, and it will mature us in the process. But perseverance will also stretch out over long seasons of quiet living when we're just working, paying our bills, loving our families, and looking for ordinary ways to make Christ known to the world around us.

For many of us, the ordinary days may outnumber the hard ones. If faithfulness grows during the challenging sea-

---

2. D. A. Carson, *Jesus' Sermon on the Mount and His Confrontation with the World: An Exposition of Matthew 5–10* (Grand Rapids, MI: Global Christian Publishing, 2001), 83–84.

sons, does that mean it lies stagnant when we're sailing along through regular life? Here's where my friend Leota showed me that following Jesus was nothing fancy yet absolutely life-changing. Regular habits of drawing near to Christ today keep us aligned with him tomorrow. And tomorrow's habits of drawing near to him will keep us near him the next day. Regardless of how yesterday looked, the gifts of grace God has given us to know and love him continually keep us by his side. Small, ordinary decisions made every day to love Jesus more, to look at him more, to cling a little tighter to him today than we did yesterday—these are the ordinary steps down the path of lifelong faithfulness.

Everyday Faithfulness Leans on God's Faithfulness

While we obey and draw near to God daily, we remember that God is the one who enables us to do so. Any white-knuckled grip we might have on Christ is born of God's own faithfulness to us. The Old Testament writers bear witness of God's faithfulness to a people who largely struggled to maintain faithfulness to him. In spite of Israel's vacillating loyalties, God loved his people with a steadfast love that was rooted in his covenant to be their God. "The steadfast love of the LORD never ceases; / his mercies never come to an end; / they are new every morning; / great is [his] faithfulness" (Lam. 3:22–23). Similarly, the New Testament writers speak of God's continual faithfulness (1 Cor. 1:9; 2 Thess. 3:3; Heb. 10:23). Though we employ the tools he's given us to remain faithful to him, it is God's faithfulness that upholds our own.

In one of Paul's prayers for the Thessalonian church, he asks that God would sanctify them and that they would be found faithful at the coming of Christ. He reminds the church that this is possible for "he who calls you is faithful; he will surely do it" (1 Thess. 5:24). Paul beseeches God himself to continue the work of sanctification in the Thessalonian believers, knowing that God's faithful character will bring about a completion of the work he had begun in the church. Paul reminded the Thessalonians that in a world of unfaithfulness, God is faithful and will "establish you and guard you against the evil one" (2 Thess. 3:3). Paul points the Thessalonian believers—and us—to the love of God and the steadfastness of Christ as the source of our endurance, the fountain from which our faithfulness flows. We persevere because God is faithful. This is a both/and process. Pastor Jeff Robinson says, "This is not to say we are passive in our perseverance. We continue trusting Christ through many dangers, toils, and snares. It is fully biblical to say both that we are persevering and also that God is preserving us."[3]

We hold fast to the means God has given us to keep believing the gospel, keep drawing near to him, and keep loving his church, knowing that obedience is the way forward. When we don't feel like it, when we're beaten down, when we feel invisible, when our time isn't our own, when we're afraid— we lean on the Lord's faithfulness to continue in our own. If you're lonely, look to God's word to know the Lord never leaves or forsakes you. Plant yourself in a body of believers who will encourage you and provide spiritual family relationships. If you're grieving or suffering physically, let the words of the Lord remind you that God will not waste your suffering but use it to refine your faith and make you more like Jesus. When you're burdened by perpetual busyness or caring for others, look for the ways you can pray while continuing in your work. Meditate on Scripture as you serve and care for children or

---

3. Jeff Robinson, "Give Us This Day Our Daily Grace," *The Gospel Coalition*, July 17, 2018, https://www.thegospelcoalition.org/article/remain-christian-hour-miracle/.

parents. Let the truths of Scripture refresh your mind when your body is weary. God has given us what we need for life and godliness. The supply never runs out!

As you persevere, be confident in the work God is doing to make your perseverance possible. Jesus is sustaining you every moment, and he will do so until you see his face. He will "sustain you to the end, guiltless in the day of our Lord Jesus Christ. God is faithful, by whom you were called into the fellowship of his Son, Jesus Christ our Lord" (1 Cor. 1:8–9). From this day until your very last day, Jesus is upholding you because God is faithful and will complete the work he began in you. You can persevere because he is preserving you.

Everyday Faithfulness Strengthens the Church

On a trip to the California coast with my sister, I had the opportunity to explore Muir Woods National Monument, a redwood forest. As we walked through the woods, my sister and I noted how the massive redwood trees grew in groves. The national park signs throughout Muir Woods didn't call them groves or circles or rings, though. The signs noted that the trees grew in families. Though they stand nearly two hundred feet tall and are often hundreds of years old, the redwoods have very shallow roots, only five or six feet deep. How could a two-hundred-foot tree that's several feet in diameter survive strong winds or flooding with only five feet of roots holding it in place? The survival of the tree depends on the family. Though the roots are shallow, they are intertwined with the roots of the other trees in the family. The tangled root system provides strength and stability for the families when nature threatens them. I was struck by how much the trees needed one another to survive. I'm not the first to make a connection between the large redwoods of California and the body of Christ, but seeing

the families of trees with my own eyes solidified my understanding of how our spiritual growth both depends upon and
contributes to the growth of others.

We've explored the ways our faithfulness is encouraged
by and through the church during various seasons of life, and
I hope you see the important role of the local church in our
perseverance. When we are discouraged, the church encourages. When we're busy, the church offers help. When we're
suffering, the church intercedes and offers care. When we're
waiting, the church helps keep our eyes on our true treasure.
When we're doubting or fighting sin, the church is engaged
in battle with us. We are not strong enough to weather the
sufferings and cares of earth on our own. The Lord knew we
would struggle. He knew we would doubt and worry and fear
and sin. He did not call us to follow him in isolation. You will
be hard-pressed to find a Christian flourishing in isolation.
That's because God designed us to need other people, and the
church is his gift to us as we seek to follow him faithfully.

We need one another—and not just in the difficult seasons. We need one another in the regular, everyday ruts of
daily living. When I look around the church sanctuary on Sunday morning and see my fellow church members singing and
listening and praying and giving, my faith is encouraged and
increased. When I listen to the friend who sits a few pews to
the right tell me about what God is teaching her in her daily
Bible reading, I am exhorted to continue in my own Bible
reading. When my Sunday school teacher tells the class about
how he's trusting the Lord in prayer over his health, my affections are stirred for the God who loves and cares for my friend.
When I meet with my church family for corporate prayer or to
study God's word together or share a meal, my roots get more
and more tangled with theirs. What binds us together is the

gospel of Jesus Christ, and because of him, our lives are all intertwined. When one is weak, the others are strong.

The opposite of all of this is also true. When the people of my church aren't fighting their sin or when they're habitually absent from corporate worship, I find myself deeply discouraged. If I'm not reading the Bible regularly or interceding for my spiritual family, what can I offer them when they are grieving or suffering? How is my root system supporting theirs if I am not feeding my own faithfulness? How is theirs supporting mine if they're not feeding their faithfulness? If we're all intertwined together, then our commitments to lifelong faithfulness depend upon one another. They need my faithfulness, and I need theirs. Paul prayed for the church to be "knit together in love" (Col. 2:2). The author of Hebrews said that meeting together regularly as the body of Christ encourages us to love and good deeds (see Heb. 10:24–25). The *togetherness* of the church keeps us growing in faith when faced with the things of earth that threaten our maturity. The tangle of roots beneath the surface grows in strength when it regularly feeds off the truth of Scripture, seeks the Lord in prayer, and spends time further knotting those roots together.

Everyday Faithfulness Is Apparent to a Watching World

When your life is built around following Christ, the people around you will know it. Unlike a room you add on to your house to make it a little bigger or more useful, Jesus isn't a helpful addition to your life. He *is* life, your entire life. Following him doesn't allow for a demarcation between the sacred and secular parts of your life. You can't compartmentalize work and worship into two different boxes; you can't file Jesus away for Sunday mornings or Wednesday evenings only. Following Christ is all-encompassing! Paul said in Colossians 3:3,

"For you have died, and your life is hidden with Christ in God." It's not our same old life with something new and interesting added on to it. No, it's a brand-new life. And that life is anchored in the person and work of Christ. "When Christ who is your life appears, then you also will appear with him in glory" (Col. 3:4). When Jesus is your life, he is your whole life, and the evidence of that will be apparent to a watching world.

A life structured around regular Scripture intake, prayer, and connection to the local church will spill over with what sustains it. Praying for your unbelieving neighbors each day will have a follow-through effect. I've found that intentional prayer for my unbelieving neighbors results in a burgeoning boldness to speak about Christ to them. When my day begins with the words of the Lord, I find the same words crowding into my conversations, whether I'm speaking with believers or unbelievers. Remaining attached to my church family has shown my unchurched friends many times over what biblical love looks like as my church has encouraged and upheld us during difficult seasons. That points them to Jesus every time. When we are constantly looking at Jesus, the unbelievers in our life will follow our gaze and see him, too.

One young couple in our church are first-generation believers in both of their families. They have constructed all of their family habits around church involvement, Bible reading, and prayer. Their extended families often complain about how saturated they are in Christianity instead of their biological family life, yet this very point of contention has given my friends ample opportunities to steer conversations to Christ. Their coworkers see their determined commitment to Christ as well, and though our young friends are regular, unremarkable folks, it is obvious to the world around them that Christ is their entire life. Their unbelieving friends and families are following their gaze and seeing Christ as the only deserving object of their affection and allegiance.

God has designed and equipped the Christian life for perseverance that reaches beyond our own benefits. In kindness, he has given us the means to accomplish his good purposes in both our lives and the lives of others as our faithfulness points others to his faithfulness. Our faithfulness isn't just for us. It announces to the world that Jesus is worth every drop of our devotion.

Everyday Faithfulness Patiently Looks to the Eternal Reward

There have been a lot of days in writing this book when I've felt my own weaknesses. I haven't obtained the kind of perseverance I aspire to—the kind I've pointed you toward for nine chapters. I know that the ordinary folks I've mentioned on these pages would say the same thing—we're not there yet. We'll never feel that we've arrived at faithfulness. But that is one of the hopeful facets of everyday faithfulness—looking forward instead of backward.

Paul expressed similar thoughts about his own walk with Christ:

> Not that I have already obtained [the resurrection] or am already perfect, but I press on to make it my own, because Christ Jesus has made me his own. Brothers, I do not consider that I have made it my own. But one thing I do: forgetting what lies behind and straining forward to what lies ahead, I press on toward the goal for the prize of the upward call of God in Christ Jesus. Let those of us who are mature think this way, and if in anything you think otherwise, God will reveal that also to you. Only let us hold true to what we have attained. (Phil. 3:12–16)

Paul encourages us to press on in everyday faithfulness, forgetting what yesterday looked like and holding fast to God's call on our life in Christ.

Spiritual maturity holds on to the future hope of being with God one day forever, fixing our eyes on what is before us. Donald Whitney says that "whether you realize it or not, everything you do is for eternity. Nothing has an impact only on this life."[4] Every morning that we wake up with breath still in our chests is an opportunity to remember our upward call of God in Christ. We move forward in daily, incremental faithfulness because Christ has made us his own. We belong to him, which means every ordinary day of perseverance belongs to him.

Paul continues in Philippians 3 to share about people he knew who had ceased following Christ in faithfulness: "For many, of whom I have often told you and now tell you even with tears, walk as enemies of the cross of Christ. Their end is their destruction, their god is their belly, and they glory in their shame, with minds set on earthly things" (Phil. 3:18–19). They held more allegiance to the world than to Christ, and it robbed them of their steadfastness. Paul reminds the Philippian believers that when the pull of the world is hard and enticing, the way forward is in setting our minds on our future hope: "But our citizenship is in heaven, and from it we await a Savior, the Lord Jesus Christ, who will transform our lowly body to be like his glorious body, by the power that enables him even to subject all things to himself. Therefore, my brothers, whom I love and long for, my joy and crown, stand firm thus in the Lord, my beloved" (Phil. 3:20–4:1). We stand firm in everyday faithfulness by fixing our gaze on our future with Christ. Our real home is coming, friend. We are sojourners passing through

---

4. Donald S. Whitney, *Spiritual Disciplines for the Christian Life* (Colorado Springs, CO: Navpress, 1991), 246.

maybe eighty years of earthbound existence. Until we reach the land of our permanent residency, we remember that it's Jesus we're persevering for and to and by and through. And he is worth every moment of our steadfastness.

Practically Speaking

Remember my failing garden? I never did try again to think like a farmer when it came to the small square of earth in my backyard. But the lessons of investment in future fruitfulness have long stayed with me. On the mornings I struggle to see merit in leaving my bed for a quiet hour of prayer and meditation on Scripture, my weedy garden comes back to me. When I want to stay home to relax rather than joining with my church family for worship or prayer, my barren tomato plants come to mind. While I haven't yet acquired a farmer's mentality in physical fruit (or vegetables), God is teaching me to think like a farmer when it comes to spiritual fruit.

James encouraged believers to consider the farmer as he watched and waited for the Lord to bring about fruit from his labors. "Be patient, therefore, brothers, until the coming of the Lord. See how the farmer waits for the precious fruit of the earth, being patient about it, until it receives the early and the late rains" (James 5:7). Patience is as necessary as labor: "You also, be patient. Establish your hearts, for the coming of the Lord is at hand" (James 5:8). But James didn't stop there with the call to think like the farmer. He also pointed believers to the prophets of old who suffered for their faithfulness to God: "As an example of suffering and patience, brothers, take the prophets who spoke in the name of the Lord. Behold, we consider those blessed who remained steadfast" (James 5:10–11). Prophets like Isaiah, Jeremiah, Hosea, and Amos encountered obstacles and suffered for the messages that God gave them to proclaim. God's call was their life, they belonged to him, and they considered the waiting and suffering worth their perseverance.

James calls us to think like farmers and live like prophets. We must work the fields and wait patiently on the Lord to bring about the fruit. Hold fast to the message of the gospel, yet expect the path before you to be difficult. Press forward because God sustains you with his own faithfulness. Embrace the ordinary days of faithfulness as they prepare you for suffering and trials. Remember that God is as invested in your sanctification as he was in your salvation. Hold on to the confession of hope that we have in Christ, and take advantage of the access to the Father that he bought for us at the cross. Whatever season or obstacle you face in this demanding world, know that you can persevere in everyday faithfulness because Christ has made you his own.

Be encouraged by John Calvin's words:

> Though severely oppressed and touched by the feeling of some bitterness, the believer, nevertheless, courageously fights that feeling and in the end perseveres. In the midst of these feelings, the endurance of the believer reveals itself. Though mercilessly provoked, the believer is nevertheless restrained by the fear of God from bursting forth in anger. In the midst of them, the steadfastness of the believer shines. Though wounded by sorrow and grief, he finds rest in the spiritual comfort of his God.[5]

---

5. A. Denlinger and B. Parson, eds., *A Little Book on the Christian Life* (Orlando, FL: Reformation Trust, 2017), 76.

Faithful Like Leota

Leota lived nearly a century as a faithful follower of Jesus. She was a wife and mother, but spent many years as a widow after her husband's death. During her retirement years, she cared for her aunt and sisters, who preceded her in death. Because she suffered from debilitating arthritis, she had to rise early on Sunday mornings to give herself plenty of time to dress and drive to church, knowing it would cost her much pain and energy to do so. She esteemed the corporate gathering of the body of Christ as more important than any other use of her time.

Leota loved to study her Bible, and she often stayed up past midnight in her recliner studying. Around the age of ninety, she began opening her home to a weekly small group meeting. Leota was remembered for her homemade fudge pies, her love of gardening, and her directness. But mostly, she was remembered for her faithfulness to Christ, her simple faith, her quiet perseverance, and her everyday faithfulness. Leota loved Jesus because she knew he loved her first. She was faithful to Christ because she knew he was faithful to her.

Acknowledgments

I'm still not a gardener. The summer that I finished this book, I let an entire herb garden wither away in thirst. Unlike my feeble attempts at cultivating food from my backyard, however, I've had lots of help in growing this book from seed to fruit. I'm indebted to those who helped in the planting and pruning of this project.

I'm grateful for Dave DeWit, who encouraged me to write this book and worked to make its publication a reality.

Special thanks to Megan Hill, whose edits and feedback were crucial in developing the early drafts of this book. Thank you for investing so much time in this project.

Many thanks to Tara Davis for helping me tighten and refine my manuscript. I'm grateful to the entire team at Crossway for believing that a book about faithfulness should be published. I'm honored to have support from the Gospel Coalition.

I could not write without the sacrifices and encouragement of my husband, William, and my sons, Isaiah and Ian. You are three of God's sweetest gifts to me, and I love that you are as excited about another book as I am.

I'm grateful for my pastors and my church family for keeping me on the path of faithfulness through prayer, accountability, encouragement, and the proclamation of God's word.

Margaret, Dorothy, Christine, Sue, Beth, Brooke, Ranelle, Dora, and Leota—thank you for pointing me to Jesus with your perseverance. I pray that those who read your stories will be encouraged to look to the Lord with confidence that he will finish the work he has begun. I'm grateful for you, my grandmothers, mothers, and sisters in the faith.

I'll never be able to adequately express my gratitude for the faithfulness of Jesus. In him, we can continue on the path of everyday faithfulness because he is our "sure and steadfast anchor of the soul" (Heb. 6:19). His death and resurrection make it possible for us to follow him faithfully until we see him face-to-face.

All glory belongs to God, who has called us to faithfulness and has made it possible in Christ.

General Index

Scripture Index

THE GOSPEL **COALITION**

The Gospel Coalition is a fellowship of evangelical churches deeply committed to renewing our faith in the gospel of Christ and to reforming our ministry practices to conform fully to the Scriptures. We have committed ourselves to invigorating churches with new hope and compelling joy based on the promises received by grace alone through faith alone in Christ alone.

We desire to champion the gospel with clarity, compassion, courage, and joy—gladly linking hearts with fellow believers across denominational, ethnic, and class lines. We yearn to work with all who, in addition to embracing our confession and theological vision for ministry, seek the lordship of Christ over the whole of life with unabashed hope in the power of the Holy Spirit to transform individuals, communities, and cultures.

Through its women's initiatives, The Gospel Coalition aims to support the growth of women in faithfully studying and sharing the Scriptures; in actively loving and serving the church; and in spreading the gospel of Jesus Christ in all their callings.

Join the cause and visit TGC.org for fresh resources that will equip you to love God with all your heart, soul, mind, and strength, and to love your neighbor as yourself.

TGC.org

Also Available from the Gospel Coalition

For more information, visit **crossway.org**.